Sheila Hutchins, who was
is the Cookery Editor of th
column every Friday. A
journalist and author, She
and cooks, in London.

Also by Sheila Hutchins

What's Cooking?
Enjoy Your Slimming (with Ann Rogers)
English Recipes and Others from Scotland, Wales and Ireland as They Appeared in Eighteenth and Nineteenth Century Cookery Books
The Daily Express Cook Book
The Daily Express Cookery Book
Your Grannie's Cook Book
Pâtés and Terrines
Good Cooking

Sheila Hutchins

Grannie's Kitchen

The North-East

MAYFLOWER
GRANADA PUBLISHING
London Toronto Sydney New York

Published by Granada Publishing Limited
in Mayflower Books 1979

ISBN 0 583 12992 7

A Mayflower UK Original

Granada Publishing Limited
Frogmore, St Albans, Herts AL2 2NF
and
3 Upper James Street, London W1R 4BP
866 United Nations Plaza, New York, NY 10017, USA
117 York Street, Sydney, NSW 2000, Australia
100 Skyway Avenue, Rexdale, Ontario, M9W 3A6, Canada
PO Box 84165, Greenside, 2034 Johannesburg, South Africa
CML Centre, Queen & Wyndham, Auckland 1, New Zealand

Set, printed and bound in Great Britain by
Cox & Wyman Ltd, Reading
Set in Intertype Times

Contents

	Introduction	9
I	Fish	15
II	Beef	31
III	Pork	47
IV	Meat of All Sorts	61
V	Brawn and the Like	75
VI	Cheese Dishes	83
VII	Sweet Puddings	91
VIII	Tarts	101
IX	High Tea	113
X	Jams, Sauces, Pickles and Vinegar	129
XI	Sweets and Toffee	137
XII	Gingerbread	147
	Index	155

Note

Both Imperial and metric weights and measures are given in this book. Either should give perfect results but they are *not* equivalents and therefore not interchangeable. Do not mix imperial and metric weights and measures in the same recipe. Use either one or the other.

Introduction

This book is written with hunger and a love of good food. Everybody knows by now that I come of an eating family. My grandfather was a brewer who lived in Blackburn, looked almost exactly like John Bull and was, so they told me, a great consumer of port and over-ripe Stilton cheese. I suppose, poor man, his only memorial would be the labels on those bottles of milk stout which were said in Victorian Lancashire not only to be good for nursing mothers but to make a man of you. But who knows what it was like now, or has ever heard of it even in Blackburn? We have forgotten so much, and are now becoming internationalized or perhaps Americanized and are losing our individuality.

The old kitchen ranges with flues and dampers and much black leading that our grannies often used required a great deal of understanding and cosseting, and when they were exchanged for gas and electricity a lot of old dishes were thrown out with them. Yet there is something extremely comforting and heart-warming about old-fashioned English food. The mere thought of boiled beef and carrots, warm and pink and trembling, with soggy onions and suet dumplings in thin clear gravy, boggles the mind and enhances the appetite, whether or not you have it with large black pickled walnuts or just a modicum of English mustard and a pint of mild and bitter.

Why does nobody care about these flavours and odours from our distant past? Why is there no monument to whoever invented bacon and eggs, no statue to steak and kidney pudding? There are memorials to moth-eaten generals and politicians, but have you ever seen a monument to Mrs Beeton, or for that matter to Mrs Raffald, perhaps the most interesting woman who ever lived in Manchester? She gave Manchester its first street directory, its first post office, ran two pubs and a confectioner's shop and opened a pleasure garden. Her cookery book, *The Experienced English Housekeeper*, published in 1769, is full of gorgeous food, much of which, apart from the antiquated language, is still very cookable. Her collared brawn is famous and, unusually for a woman in those days, she could both read and write and also spoke French. Femininity, however, overcame her in the end, for after having sixteen children she died at the age of forty-eight in childbirth.

This book is largely full of recipes that I have collected in different parts of the north country during the past thirty years when writing my weekly cookery column for the *News Chronicle*, and later the *Daily Herald* and *The Sun* and then the *Daily Express.*

I have always thought that there were hundreds of marvellous old dishes in Britain that are gradually being forgotten; wonderful things that your granny and my granny used to cook and if we are going to save these things we shall have to do it quickly. When I said this in print I got thousands of recipes from all over Britain. I had letters from retired cooks, former kitchen maids in great country houses, farmers' wives, great-aunts and grandmothers, some in spidery copper-plate handwriting. I had letters from men as well as women, sailors, Chelsea Pensioners, whelk-fishermen, eel-jelliers and asparagus-growers. They speak in many different voices with many different accents and most of the recipes have their own regional flavour. At times it was as if you could hear the whole of England chewing.

Some of the recipes were published by the *Daily Express* in 'Your Grannie's Cook Book' about seven years ago and the Editor has kindly allowed me to reprint a few of them here. But there are other recipes in this book that you are unlikely to find elsewhere.

Some readers sent me whole handwritten cookery books and there are memories of hot dinners from long-distant childhoods, of old brick ovens and black-leaded coal ranges. I have sometimes had letters from abroad including Australia and New Zealand. Once I wrote in my column that the famous Granny Smith apple came from a tree planted by English settlers about eighty years ago in an Australian garden and that nobody now remembered who they were. I then received a fascinating letter from some people living near Birmingham who wrote that Granny Smith was also *their* granny and that it was *their* relatives who had gone to Australia and planted the apple tree.

There are recipes and reminiscences in this book from my own north-country childhood and when I realize that most people nowadays have never even heard of a dolly mangle I begin to suspect that it was some time ago. And I have sometimes wondered, if it is true that a drowning man sees all his past life surge before him, unrolling chapter by chapter in the mind's eye, how much of mine would consist of a succession of hot dinners. And whether a ghostly odour of fried onions would float across the briny deep. I fancy that in extreme old age I may even discuss culinary victories – just as retired generals in bathchairs are said to talk of battles long ago; the eggs I have beaten, the sauces reduced . . . the lunches I have eaten, the dishes I have cooked.

I
Fish

Whitby Lobsters
Hot Lobster and Butter
Kippers
Cold Cod Steaks in Lemon Sauce
Sea Houses
Home-made Potted Crab
Scarborough Cod
Boiled Cod and Melted Butter
Kipper Soufflé
Hull Fish Cakes
Baked Staithes Herrings
Potted Shrimps
Flat-Fish and Shrimps
Fish Hot-Pot
Mackerel
Fried Herrings
Grilled Herrings
Salmon Scouse
Tweed Salmon
Trout and Salmon
To Pot Salmon
Char

Fish

The North Sea herring fishing is not what it was, for the fish are scarce and have largely left the North Sea and the catch is restricted. But when the herring 'rises' Whitby always becomes extremely busy. The local fleet is, traditionally, joined by about a hundred Scottish herring boats, as well as Dutch, German and other foreign boats which can usually be seen lying alongside each other after a night at sea. During the herring season Whitby is mostly packed tight with fishing boats, so many that sometimes one could almost walk across the harbour on their decks. In summer, when the herring fleet is in port and the harbour is full, the impressive service of the 'blessing of the boats' takes place from the fish pier.

The women of Whitby still knit sweaters in traditional patterns for the fishermen. Which pattern you wear depends on which family you belong to and local families wear their ancestrally-patterned sweaters with pride. They have a sinister origin, however, for ultimately the pattern on the sweater is to enable the corpse of a man drowned at sea to be identified when washed up, even if it is otherwise unrecognizable.

Whitby is on a wild and dangerous part of the Yorkshire coast, with beautiful sunsets caused partly by the sea 'fret' or mist that lies across the coast in haunted-looking patches. The traditional North Sea fishing cobles and keel boats are still built in the harbour and there is a swing bridge that opens to let the timber ships go up river to the docks.

In the nineteenth century it was a base for whaling ships and the blubber was unloaded into boiler houses on the quays. Captain William Scoresby who caught 533 whales and invented the 'crow's nest' was a famous Whitby man. The fishermen are very superstitious and one must not go out to sea with the hatches upside down, nor mention pigs in Whitby. You have to call them grunters, or rats, otherwise it is very unlucky.

When I was there about ten years ago people kept talking to me about Old Misser, the wassel-cup singer who died a few years back. She wore a black shawl and 'looked like a witch'. If the men saw her they would not go out fishing. She used to have 'pot dolls hidden in a basket on her arm'. The men would give her five or even ten shillings to get rid of her, for fear of being ill-looked.

Whitby Lobsters

You can buy delicious Whitby-smoked kippers in the town and Whitby fishermen export live lobsters to Paris. One sees scores of them on the quays being packed up to go to France and there are special sea tanks for 'hullying' them, or sprucing them up for the journey. When alive, lobsters are, of course, bright blue not red, and they are often full of berries (the eggs or coral) which, when raw, are black. They say in Whitby that lobster berries are better than caviar. Some of the men like to take them off in handfuls and eat them on the quay.

Hot Lobster and Butter

One of the simplest and most delicious ways of serving a hot, freshly-boiled lobster is with warm melted butter, just mixed with the juice of half a lemon and a little salt and pepper. A more elaborate sauce sometimes disguises the flavour. Nothing else is needed, except perhaps some thin brown bread and butter and a bottle of white wine, even perhaps some fresh-pulled new potatoes as a supplementary pleasure.

Kippers

A delicious way of cooking kippers for breakfast from Mrs Scott of Sea Breeze in Blackpool, Lancashire. Stand a colander over a pan of boiling water, spread a piece of foil in it. Lay the kippers on it. Cover them with the pan lid and let them steam for 6–8 minutes. Serve them with any liquid that has collected in the foil poured over them.

Mrs Scott also says that kipper fillets can just be unwrapped, but left in the cellophane wrapper, laid flat in the colander with the kipper fillets on top, and cooked in the same way.

Cold Cod Steaks in Lemon Sauce

This is served garnished with capers and parsley. Put *a large peeled sliced onion,* 1 *teaspoon salt and* ¼ *teaspoon white pepper* in a pan with 375*ml* (¾ *pint*) *water* and 3 *tablespoons sugar* (it improves the flavour of the fish!). Bring to the boil.

Rinse 4 *cod steaks of about* 100*g* (4 *oz*) *each.* Salt them. Lower them into the hot liquid (on a sling made of cooking foil if liked. This makes it much easier to lift them out in one piece when cooked). Let them simmer, poaching and just bubbling very, very gently for 20 minutes – the water should tremble rather than boil. Take them out, put them on a serving dish, removing the skins when they are cold.

To make the sauce, beat 2 *large eggs* with the strained *juice of* 2 *lemons* and gradually whisk in 250*ml* (1 *pt*) of strained fish stock. Pour this into the top of a double pan with hot, but not quite boiling, water in the pan below. Heat gently, stirring all the time, until it thickens like a coating custard.

If it boils the eggs will scramble and the sauce will be ruined. When the sauce has thickened, pour it over the fish to coat it completely and leave it in a cool larder overnight. Halibut, turbot and even conger eel can be cooked like this.

Sea Houses

This is a small fishing village in Northumberland with a regular boat service in summer to the Farne Islands, where the grey seals breed; Grace Darling, who made her famous rescue in 1838, was the lighthouse keeper there. And it was at Sea Houses that kippers were invented. John Woodger adapted the method of kippering salmon to kipper local herring in the mid-nineteenth century, splitting them down the back, soaking them in brine and then smoking them over oak sawdust. The fishing village of Craster further along the Northumbrian coast is also famous for its pale juicy kippers. These are smoked in season in the old-fashioned way from June to September. One can get them by writing to: L. Robson and Sons, Fish Curers, Craster, Northumberland.

The fishing cobles at Sea Houses mostly go after crabs and lobsters, and in this part of England the lobster pots are quite unlike those basket affairs used in Cornwall and the South. They are rectangular, partly of metal, and look more like huge rat-traps. Until recently in Northumberland, as in Scotland, only the legs and claws of crabs were eaten, the rest being thought unwholesome. Crab and shrimp teas are, however, one of the features of the English seaside and in country districts, particularly in the North, no high tea is complete without Crab Paste, or Potted Crab, to eat with hot buttered toast.

Home-made Potted Crab

Take the meat from 3 *freshly-cooked medium crabs*, cracking the shell where necessary, keeping the white meat from the claws and so on, separate from the yellow crumbly part, of course, you must first remove the grey banana-shaped lungs inside the shell, the small papery sac behind the eyes and all green matter. Mash or pound each to a fine texture, but not a paste, adding *a little freshly-grated nutmeg* and *a small pinch of curry powder* to each, with the strained *juice of a lemon* and *a little melted butter*. Pack the crab meat in small white potting pots in layers, covering these with clarified butter to seal them from the air. It keeps quite well in the fridge for about a week or for longer in the freezer.

Scarborough Cod

Genuine fresh cod should have a bluish-white belly and a greenish tinge on its back, with the skin glistening. It is at its best in winter and that caught off Scarborough is said to be the finest in the country.

The taste of a piece of plainly-poached newly-caught cod, not more than one or two hours out of the sea, is one that we have almost forgotten. If you go down to any of the fishing ports in winter – North Shields, Fleetwood, Grimsby or Hull – you can see them fresh out of the water, green as a mermaid and long as an umbrella, and totally different from the wet-flannel-type of frozen fish fillet. Those are from fish caught in distant waters, gutted at sea and stored in ice for anything up to three weeks before the trawlers even get to port. They make good fish pie and so on but are a very different thing.

Boiled Cod and Melted Butter

Unless you live in a fishing port you may have to catch the fish yourself off the end of the pier to get it fresh enough for this dish. It is served with floury boiled potatoes cooked Lancashire style and a jug of hot frothing melted butter.

Get your fish, fresh caught in the morning, put it under ice-cold running water and leave it there for some hours until ready to cook it. This revives it like a lettuce. Drain the fish just before the meal. Sprinkle it thick with *salt* and leave it for 15–20 minutes before rinsing and cooking it. For this, take a large pan of boiling water with 2 *tablespoons vinegar* and 40*g* (1½ *oz*) *salt per litre* (2 *pts*) *of water.* Into it lower 1.25*kg* (3 *lb*) *of best line-caught Scarborough cod* cut in 4cm (1½ in) thick steaks. Bring water and fish gently to the boil, skimming off the froth. Turn off the heat and put a lid tightly on the pan. Let the pan of fish and water stand on the stove for about 10 minutes.

Serve the drained cod steaks in a folded napkin. The fish should lie in broad chalk-white flakes, almost crisp. Have ready a jug with 100–150*g* (4–6 *oz*) *melted butter* and *a finely-chopped hard-boiled egg* in it. Also mustard sauce if liked. Pale ale goes very well with this. This dish is also popular in Scandinavia and is eaten in Denmark on New Year's Day when they also serve cod's roes and cod's livers boiled separately, with it.

Kipper Soufflé

Some of the boarding houses and small hotels in Douglas make a speciality of Hot Kipper Soufflé prepared with those superb local Manx kippers. The kippers are world famous, exported even to the United States, and north-country people who go to the Isle of Man on holiday during Wakes Week make a point of sending some home to their friends. They are especially delicate because they are smoked over oak sawdust and because Manx law forbids the use of artificial dyes in preparing them. They are pale lemon in colour.

For the soufflé put 3 *kippers* in a jug. Pour in boiling water to come right up to the tails. Leave them about 5 minutes. Lift them out, skin and bone them, being careful to get rid of even the very tiny bones. Mash the flesh. Take 2 *tablespoons of milk* and use it to mix 20*g* (¾ *oz*) *cornflour* to a smooth paste. Bring 375*ml* (¾ *pt*) *milk* to the boil, stir in the cornflour mixture. Cook, stirring for 5 minutes. Add the mashed kipper and *a little pepper and nutmeg*. Salt will not be necessary. Remove from the heat and when cool stir in 2 *beaten egg yolks* and heat, stirring until the mixture thickens a little.

Beat 3 *egg whites* so stiff that the basin may be turned upside down without them falling out. Fold them into the kipper mixture, pour it *at once* into a buttered soufflé dish. Bake it *at once* in a hot oven, 200°C (400°F) Gas Mark 6 for about 20 minutes. Eat it *at once*. Soufflés go flat if they have to wait.

Hull Fish Cakes

'I am fortunate because my husband brings me fresh fish from the Hull dock each week,' Mrs Shirley Close, of Kirk-ella in East Yorkshire, wrote to me about six years ago. 'This has been a favourite recipe ever since my father and his father sailed on the Hull trawlers.'

Skin and flake *about* 400*g* (1 *lb*) *cooked haddock or cod* and mix it well with about 400*g* (1 *lb*) *creamed potatoes.* Add *a beaten egg, a good squeeze of lemon juice, salt and pepper* and *a pinch of mixed herbs* and beat well. Shape into 'cakes' on a floured board, brush with *egg* and cover them with *breadcrumbs.* Fry them in hot fat for a few minutes on each side.

Baked Staithes Herrings

Staithes is a storm-battered fishing port on the Yorkshire coast, fiercely independent and where some of the fish wives still wear traditional white cotton bonnets when skeyning mussels and gutting fish. The village is down a hill marked 1 in 4 that looks even steeper. It was the birthplace of Captain Cook and, in the nineteenth century, the home of one or two artists – but they risked being pelted with fish heads if seen painting on a Sunday. Staithes speech is full of old Viking words and the local people can understand the Danish seamen on the timber boats. But when I was there I could not find anyone to take me out in a lobster boat as they said it is unlucky to have a woman aboard.

First, clean and fillet *one herring per person,* then lay the herrings flat out on the table, skin side down, sprinkling them with *pepper and salt and chopped fresh mint.* Put *a slice of onion* chopped up on each one, before you roll them up and put them in a greased pie dish to bake, first in a hot oven, 200°C (400°F) Gas Mark 6, for 5 minutes. Then reduce the heat to moderately slow 170°C (300°F) Gas Mark 3, and cook them for nearly half an hour.

They are delicious either hot or cold and you mop up the

gravy with brown bread and butter. Some cooks mix *a beaten egg* with *a tablespoon of water* and *a tablespoon of vinegar* and pour this over the rolled-up herrings before baking. Either way is good.

These are first cousins to the *maquereaux au vin blanc* so popular as 'starters' in all the northern French fishing ports.

Potted Shrimps

The best potted shrimps are said to come from Parkgate in Cheshire. The shrimps are caught near where Mary used to call the cattle home across the sands of Dee. There used to be little seaside cottages with freshly-baked bread, salty Cheshire butter and perhaps honeycomb mould where you could have shrimp teas, with delicious shrimp paste as well as potted shrimps. There were places, too, where, if you left £1 and your name and address, they would send a succession of potted shrimps after you by post for the rest of the summer.

Of course, those of the Morecambe Bay are close rivals. There is a flat sandy coast there, too, where the sea goes out for miles and shrimps are caught from horse-drawn carts fitted with nets.

There were two kinds of potted shrimps: those which were cooked, peeled, seasoned and set solid in a jar then topped with clarified butter, and another which was really a pink shrimp paste which sometimes had tinned salmon as well as whole peeled shrimps in it. This had butter on top too.

In Morecambe Bay the vast sands can be crossed at low tide if you stick to the proper routes. (What happens if you stray I have never known but death by quicksands or drowning has always seemed to me inevitable.) Kent's Bank, in Cartmel I think, was the northern end of the mule route across Morecambe which was used by stage-coaches as well as men on horseback before the coming of steam.

To pot shrimps melt 200g (8 *oz*) *unsalted or very lightly-salted butter* (or clarified butter) in a pan, adding ¾ *tea-*

spoon freshly-grated nutmeg, some *freshly-ground black pepper* and a *small pinch of Cayenne pepper.* Add 200*g* (8 *oz*) *peeled shrimps* and cook them gently, stirring from time to time, for almost 5 minutes. Take the pan off the heat and taste for seasoning. Adjust if necessary. Spoon the shrimps and butter into small pots (such as ramekins or *cocottes* to hold enough for one person), the butter must cover them completely. Add more melted butter at the end if need be. Cool them quickly, cover, seal, freeze. Before serving, thaw them at room temperature for about four hours. Serve them in the individual pots with lemon wedges, thin brown bread and butter for 'starters' at a dinner party. If more convenient, freeze them in small cartons such as cream or yogurt cartons then turn them out, frozen, on a dish to serve after letting them thaw.

Flat-Fish and Shrimps

Smear 25*g* (1 *oz*) *butter* thickly all over a shallow oven-proof dish with your fingers. Add *salt and pepper* then the *flash fish – whole plaice, flounders or lemon sole* black side down, having slashed it right down the back bone so it cooks more quickly. Top it with *potted shrimps* and the shrimp butter. Cover with buttery paper. Bake it in a moderate oven, 180°C (350°F) Gas Mark 4, for almost 30 minutes depending on the thickness of the fish. It is done if the plain end of a match-stick goes in easily through the thickest part. Meanwhile beat up 1 *egg* in 250*ml* (½ *pt*) *very thick cream,* add *salt and pepper,* and heat stirring gently without actually letting it boil as it would curdle. Then pour off the buttery juices from the baking dish, stirring them into the hot cream. Pour this over the fish. Brown it under the grill if you like.

Fish Hot-Pot

Almost any white fish is good when cooked with onions but when I lived in Cheshire the fish used to come up from Mr

Stanway's shop in Northwich via a boy on a bicycle. He wore a long blue and white striped cotton coat like a heavy overall, and a straw boater in fine weather. *Chunks of cod, hake, whole haddocks*, or *a series of cod steaks*, were seasoned with *salt, pepper* and *a very little dry mustard powder*, then put in a fire-proof dish with *melted butter* poured over it. The fish was browned lightly in a moderate oven 180°C (350°F) Gas Mark 4, then surrounded with *raw potatoes* cut in rounds as for a hot-pot. They were mixed with 3 *or* 4 *raw sliced onions*, salt and pepper and some *chopped parsley*. The vegetables were sprinkled with melted butter and it was all put back in the oven for 30–40 minutes until the potatoes were cooked. It was served, sprinkled with more chopped parsley, in the baking dish.

Mackerel

'My husband is a wholesale fish merchant and as you can imagine I've cooked and eaten nearly every fish in the sea; cod – hake – gurnet – bream – brill – turbot – plaice – ray backs – ray patches – conger eel – salmon – trout – hatchet – megs – ling – coley – monk fish – squid – dog fish – cat fish – sturgeon – grilse – sword fish – haddock – herrings – mackerel – whiting – white bait – rock salmon – etc., etc., etc. I have cooked all these fish in emergency, you can imagine. And the one I like the best, my husband calls it the scavenger of the seas, is mackerel.

'I oil the bottom of my grill pan and lay in the *boned fillets of mackerel*. I spread them liberally with *made mustard*, and a little *brown caster sugar*, then knobs of *butter*. On the top grill for 15–20 minutes. Serve with garden peas (frozen), chips and *apple sauce* or my special mustard sauce:

'1 *medium-sized onion* finely-chopped, 1 *large teaspoon powdered mustard*, 1 *to* 4 *teaspoons sugar* and mix it together with *salad cream or mayonnaise* to a slightly thick consistency. Delicious.'

The fascinating fish list and the recipe are from Mrs Doris Randall of Thornton Cleveleys in Lancashire.

Fried Herrings

Clean the fish. Take out the backbone if you prefer to. Wash the *herrings* well and let them drain. Toss them in *seasoned flour* and fry them about 4 minutes per side until golden brown. They are very good with brown bread and butter, a pot of freshly-made tea and some mustard sauce (see page 50).

To flour the herrings it is easiest to put the flour, salt and pepper in a paper bag then shake the prepared fish in this, one by one, to coat them before frying, preferably in a mixture of oil and butter, though pork dripping is also delicious.

Grilled Herrings

Clean and scale the *herrings*, cutting off their heads, but do not split them. Make three slanting cuts on each side of each fish. Heat the grill, lining the wire rack with buttered foil, so they will not stick. The foil also prevents the grill from smelling fishy afterwards. A little mustard powder in the washing up water is helpful, too.

Grill them 3–4 minutes per side. Serve piping hot, garnished with *parsley*. Washed, boiled potatoes are good with them, too, and a squeeze of lemon juice.

Salmon Scouse

This is an old Lakeland dish. It is simply freshly-steamed *salmon*, skinned, boned and mixed with very buttery well-seasoned *mashed potatoes*. This is served with a traditional *hot egg sauce* – a rich white sauce with a number of chopped hard-boiled eggs in it.

Tweed Salmon

In some northern country houses fried salmon steaks are still eaten at breakfast, and in Northumberland there used to be a most unusual way of cooking salmon from the celebrated border river Tweed, in a hot marinade or pickle.

The *salmon steaks* are first poached in lightly-salted water just to cover them. It is enough to bring this water with the fish gently to the boil then the pan is removed from the heat and the fish is allowed to get cold in the liquor, or 'dover', as they say in Northumberland. The pieces of salmon are put in a deep serving dish with *a little freshly-grated nutmeg, ground cloves* and *freshly-milled pepper*. Equal amounts of *white wine*, the fish dover and *white wine vinegar* are added. The salmon is left in it to marinate for about 24 hours. Then it is served hot, heated in the liquor. We have not tried this delicate old recipe yet.

Trout and Salmon

Sea trout and salmon are caught in the river Lune around Kirkby Lonsdale. Yorkshire is full of trout streams, Driffield Beck being a famous one. Some grayling is also caught and Isaak Walton and his friend Charles Cotton used to fish for trout in the river Dove in Derbyshire.

TO FRY PERCH OR TROUT 'When you have scaled, gutted and washed your perch or trout, dry them well, then lay them separately on a board before the fire. Two minutes before you fry them dust them well with flour, and fry them a fine brown in roast drippings or rendered suet. Serve them up with melted butter or crisped parsley.
From THE EXPERIENCED ENGLISH HOUSEKEEPER by Elizabeth Raffald, Manchester 1769.

Pork or bacon drippings are in fact delicious for cooking brook trout. The 'melted butter' is not what it seems but was a sauce very popular in England in the eighteenth century and not unlike a *sauce hollandaise* or more accurately the *beurre blanc* of the river Loire in France.

Mrs Raffald's book is dedicated to the Hon. Lady Elizabeth Warburton of Arley Hall, Cheshire, for whom she worked as housekeeper, marrying the gardener in 1763 and giving birth, during the next eighteen years, to sixteen daughters. During this time this amazing north-country woman not only looked after a celebrated confectionery shop at Fennel Street in Manchester but ran three Lancashire inns, wrote her best-selling and excellent cookery book, established the first post office in Manchester, published a street directory – something like the Parisian *Didot Bottin* – and also ran an employment agency for women. As far as we are aware there is no memorial to her in Manchester.

To Pot Salmon

'When you have any cold salmon left, take the skin off, and bone it. Then put it in a marble mortar, with a good deal of clarified butter. Season it pretty high with pepper, mace and salt, shred a little fennel very small. Beat them all together exceeding fine, then put it close down into a pot, and cover it with clarified butter.'

From THE EXPERIENCED ENGLISH HOUSEKEEPER, by Elizabeth Raffald, Manchester 1769.

Char

This deep water fish is found in Lake Windermere as well as in some fathomless Welsh lakes. Though not especially prized here now, and almost unknown, it is a sort of Golden Alpine trout, served as a special dish in some lakeside hotels in Austria (where it is called *Seibling*) as well as in Scandinavia. This is the same fish as the *omble chevalier* so much esteemed in France that they serve it at State banquets. It is caught in Lake Geneva, or was, before pollution reduced its numbers. Around Lake Annecy it is so highly valued that an extensive and very costly programme has been undertaken to clean the lake waters and prevent further pollution. Now gin clear, they are a great source of local pride and the *omble chevalier* from Lake Annecy is said to have a finer flavour than any other.

Char, or *omble chevalier*, is in season in Britain from July to October.

Though little sought after in Britain, char was once a feature of leading hotels in the Lake District where it was potted, or made into enormous pies, or eaten freshly-caught. It was a well-known delicacy in Queen Anne's day, too, when 'the fish called charr came potted to London'.

II
Beef

Roast Rump of Beef and Yorkshire Pudding
Yorkshire Pudding
Traditional Yorkshire Pudding
Yorkshire Pudding with Mushrooms
Beef Pot Roast and Forcemeat Balls or Mock Jugged Hare
Stewed Rump of Beef
Balmbra's Pudding
Basso Profundo
Yorkshire Cobbler
Alice's Rich Beef Pie
Rump Steak and Onions
Salted Dry-Fried Steaks
Beef Sausages
Panakelty
Dripping Toast and Chip Butties

Beef

In the days before kitchen ranges when people cooked on the open hearth, the Sunday joint, usually beef, was often cooked in the baker's oven and used to be taken, with the accompanying Yorkshire pudding in a jug, to the baker on the way to church. Of course most people could not afford roast beef, certainly not every Sunday, and it must have been fetched home with pride and carried high and haughty through the village.

It is a matter of family pride in the north to have four or even five different vegetables with the joint. They are usually plain boiled and home grown, and some put butter on them and some do not. Then in Lancashire people are especially fussy about the way the potatoes are cooked and to my mind Lancashire women are often even better potato cooks than the Irish themselves. Apart from the accompanying vegetables there are also all those delicious extras which are sometimes served before the joint and sometimes with it. They are among the glories of our national cooking and especially popular in the North.

In Northumberland superb home-made pease pudding is eaten with roasts, as well as with boiled hams and a whole gamut of meat dishes. There are parsley dumplings and hot leek puddings. In Yorkshire there are delicious savoury and season puddings as well as the Yorkshire pudding we all know.

There is an excellent suet pudding stuffed with mushrooms, that is eaten with a rich gravy before the roast and in Cumberland they used to make a herb pudding in spring from chopped green herbs, cooked barley, butter and an egg; this was steamed in a pudding basin and was eaten with underdone roast beef. People often blame the housewife for her ignorance in not knowing the names of the different cuts of meat, but this is hardly fair. Meat is cut differently in different parts of the country and the names of the actual cuts vary too.

In the North of England for instance you might find Silverside called Round of Beef in Durham and Topside called Insteak. In Yorkshire, Silverside is popularly known as a Salmon Cut. A shoulder cut of beef is named Ribraff in Halifax whilst the same cut is called Palo Bono in Barnsley; in Sheffield the Soft End of Bed Piece would also be Silverside; in North Yorkshire the Thin Rib is sometimes referred to as the Garden Gate. Fillet Steak is called Queen's Beet in Newcastle; in Liverpool, Shin is known by the local name of Off the Off Meat; in Leeds, Blade of Pork might be referred to as Spur; a Navvy's Waistcoat could be Breast of Lamb in Cheshire; in Blackburn you might find Thick Rib of Lamb called Heater End, Brisket called Nose-end and Quarter Beef, Rib and Chuck named Garden Gate. In Rochdale, Hockle refers to the Shin, in Bradford, Butcher's Apron would mean Breast of Lamb and Runner would refer to Rib. Bacon Ribs are locally known as Spare Ribs in Liverpool; in Leeds, Belly of Pork may be called Draught; in York you could find Belly Pork Fat called Mudgeon Fat, Veiling or Scratcheons.

Roast Rump of Beef and Yorkshire Pudding

Mr J. W. Hebden is a family butcher, his shop is at Cracoe, a few miles outside Skipton, one of the old cattle-market towns with a moated castle overlooking the High Street. He is known over a large part of Yorkshire not only for his hams, sausages, pickled tongues and lovely bacon but for the very high quality of the meat he sells.

It is always fascinating, I think, to know what the experts themselves eat, and this is what he told me: 'One meal which we regularly enjoy is not fancy in any way but very tasty. It is Yorkshire Pudding (which of course is served first and separately on its own) followed by a piece of Rump of Beef. This is covered in foil, put into a roasting tin (covered) with a small amount of water and cooked – not so long per pound but until the fork goes through!

'When ready, the juices are thickened into a gravy which is of course served first with the Yorkshire Pudding. A choice of veg such as turnip, steeped peas or sprouts, roast or mashed potatoes, or, for a change, jacket potatoes. This is followed often by a milk pudding such as rice or sago.'

Rump of Beef (Fr. *culotte de boeuf*) is the next joint to topside, not quite so lean and therefore more succulent, usually very good value. When from a good butcher it is absolutely delicious roasted in foil, a modern idea which is becoming more and more popular. The foil keeps the oven clean, protects the meat from drying (like the fat tied round veal, and so on, in France) and the moist heat also tenderizes the meat. Most people remove the foil for the last 20–30 minutes to let the meat brown. When using foil, or a covered roasting tin (which serves the same purpose) it is best to have a fairly hot oven 190°C–200°C (375°F–400°F) Gas Mark 5–6, as the covering deflects some of the heat. The potatoes then brown well, too, in dripping in a separate tin.

When a roast is cooked it is a good idea to let the meat stand for 15 minutes on its hot dish, by the open oven, to 'set' ready for carving. This is done while one is dishing up or while eating the Yorkshire Pudding.

'Another tasty mid-week meal' Mr Hebden added, 'is – 1 *cow-heel*, 1 *oxtail*, 400g (1 *lb*) *shin of beef*. Cut up and cook all these together and when ready remove all the bones and serve the meat hot with the veg of your choice.' As Mr Hebden says, 'Any meat remaining can be pressed into a mould and used cold as a potted meat.'

Yorkshire Pudding

There are almost as many old family recipes for Yorkshire Pudding as there are cooks, and almost any North Country housewife knows 'the only correct way' of cooking it. I have heard Yorkshiremen say it is made quite differently in Dewsbury from Huddersfield for instance.

This is the way it was made at home in my childhood, my mother must have had the recipe from her home in Blackburn, Lancashire.

Mix 100*g* (4 *oz*) *flour*, 1 *teaspoon salt* and 2 *eggs* in a big pancake bowl adding enough *milk and water* – half and half to make a beating consistency. Beat the batter well as you add the liquid little by little, beating out any lumps as you do so. Season it with *salt and pepper*. Add the rest of the liquid to make 250ml (½ pt) altogether. Let the batter stand for 30 minutes after beating it.

You must have some very hot fat – not too much of it – and a nice hot oven. Get the dripping hot in a roasting tin and pour in the batter and put it in the oven 30 minutes before the joint is done, raising this on a rack above it. The batter absorbs the taste of the beef fat dripping on to it in cooking.

TRADITIONAL YORKSHIRE PUDDING This is a recipe from Ingleby Arncliffe Women's Institute which was given in the 1927 edition of Yorkshire Recipes from the Y.F.W.I. at Rechabite Building in Clifford Street, York.

'Put 6 tablespoons of flour and a pinch of salt into a basin, make a hole in the middle into which pour a little milk. Break in two eggs and beat into a smooth batter and then thin down with a little water.

'The joint to be eaten with Yorkshire pudding must be roasted before the fire. Place a shallow baking tin under the joint to catch the dripping. When dripping and tin are quite hot, pour in the batter. When browned on one side, cut in squares and turn. In winter two tablespoons of snow can be used instead of eggs. In this case the batter will be slightly whiter.'

Yorkshire Pudding with Mushrooms

This delicious recipe was once given to me by Mr Price who used to sell bicycle parts, radios, torch batteries and fireworks in what used, in my childhood, to be the smithy in Davenham village in Cheshire.

Fry 100*g or* 200*g* (4 *or* 8 *oz*) *mushrooms* in lard or dripping. Make your Yorkshire Pudding by putting 3 *large heaped tablespoons flour* into a basin, *add salt,* stir in 250*ml* (½ *pt*) *milk* to make it all smooth and add 3 *eggs* well beaten in 125*ml* (¼ *pt*) *milk.* Beat the mixture well and let it stand for about an hour. Put the mushrooms and batter in a shallow baking tin well-rubbed with beef dripping and bake it in a moderate oven 180°C (350°F) Gas Mark 4 for a good half hour.

It tastes even better cooked under the joint. Stand this on the bars of the oven or on a tall wire rack and let the juices and fat drip into the tin underneath. About half an hour before it is done, pour off the surplus fat. Leave a little in the tin, put in the mushrooms and batter and proceed as above letting the joint go on dripping over it till it's time for Sunday dinner.

Beef Pot Roast and Forcemeat Balls or Mock Jugged Hare

'Mock Jugged Hare was a great favourite of my grandmother in Yorkshire in the eighteen hundred and nineties,' as Mrs C. Williamson of Thornham, Rochdale, Lancashire, wrote to me some years back. 'She lived on a farm and had to feed the farm men in addition to her own family. In those days shin beef was very cheap; it, of course, required cooking for several hours but as a coal oven in an old-fashioned range was used it did not involve much expense.'

The meat is, in fact, pot roasted or braised in an earthenware or metal casserole with a well-fitting lid, and is very suitable for those with a solid fuel cooker. No liquid is added, the meat cooks in its own juice and that of the vegetables with it, but the lid must fit tightly.

Cut 800*g* (2 *lb*) shin beef in pieces about the size of a joint of hare, flour it well, and braise it until brown in some good *beef dripping* in the frying-pan. Then put it in a brown earthenware dish, with 2 *peeled whole onions* with 4 *cloves stuck in each,* some *strips of lemon rind, mixed herbs* and *seasoning*, and a foil top or well-fitting lid. Cook it in a slow oven 170°C (325°F) Gas Mark 3 for 3–4 hours. Strain off the gravy and thicken it by stirring in *a little flour*. Keep stirring until the gravy is smooth, thick, and does not taste floury. Arrange the meat on a serving dish and pour the gravy over it. Discard the onions. Serve it with red-currant jelly and forcemeat balls.

FOR THE FORCEMEAT BALLS Mix together 5 *tablespoons soft white breadcrumbs*, 50*g* (2 *oz*) *chopped suet*, 1 *teaspoon parsley*, ½ *teaspoon mixed herbs*, ½ *teaspoon grated lemon rind*, some *salt and pepper*. Mix it all well together.

Roll into little balls with floured hands, put some beef dripping in a roasting tin, heat this in the oven, then add the forcemeat balls and roast them for 30 minutes, turning them over as they brown. They are best cooked in a moderate oven 180°C (350°F) Gas Mark 4 but, of course, if the heat is slightly lower, they will take a little longer.

Stewed Rump of Beef

'When I was a little girl and my granny invited the family over for dinner, I was allowed to go very early to help her prepare the meal,' Mrs Meaghan, of Chorley, Lancashire, once wrote to me. 'When the rest of my family arrived later and I opened the door for them I used to watch their faces as the delicious smell from the kitchen met them. Now I get the same looks on my own family's face when I am making granny's Stewed Rump of Beef.

'Wash a *rump of beef* well and season with *pepper, Cayenne, salt, cloves* and *mace* in fine powder. Bind it up tight and place it in a pot. Fry 3 *large onions*, sliced, and add them to the pan with 3 *carrots, a turnip, a shallot*, 4 *cloves, a blade of mace* and some *celery*. Cover the meat with a good *beef broth or weak gravy*. Simmer it gently for several hours till quite tender. Clear off the fat and add to the gravy 250*ml* (½ *pt*) *port wine* and a *small glass of vinegar*, also *a large spoon of ketchup*. Simmer for 30 minutes and serve in a deep dish. Garnish with carrots, turnips or pickles cut small and laid in little heaps separately. If, when done, the gravy is too much to fill the dish take only a part to season for serving. A spoonful of made mustard is a great improvement to the gravy.'

Balmbra's Pudding

Balmbra's is a famous old pub and music hall in the Cloth Market in Newcastle and it was from here – according to the celebrated song that is now almost the Geordie anthem – that they all set out to go to Blaydon Races:

'Aa went to Blaydon Races,
'twas on the ninth of June,
Eighteen hundred and sixty two
on a summer's afternoon.
Aa tyuk the bus fra Balmbra's
and she was heavy laedn.
Away we went alang Collingwood Street
that's on the road to Blaydon.'

Mr Keith Wilson who does the music-hall promotions at Balmbra's has given me this delicious recipe. As he says himself, it is a combination of two Northumbrian dishes, Leek Pudding and Steak and Kidney Pudding.

Put 200*g* (8 *oz*) *flour* (with 12*g* (½ *oz*) of baking powder if plain) in a basin with a *teaspoon of salt* and 4–6 *well-washed green leek leaves, finely chopped.* Mix them all well together then rub in 75*g* (3 *oz*) beef fat – either suet or dripping. Moisten this with enough cold water to make a stiff dough.

Roll it out nearly 12mm (½ in) thick. Use it to line a greased 1kg (2 lb) pudding basin, leaving enough dough to fold over the top of the filling and to seal the filled basin.

Peel 2 *large onions*, chop them into 6mm (¼ in) dice. Set them to stew with 200*g* (8 *oz*) *diced stewing steak* and 100*g* (4 *oz*) *chopped ox kidney*, season this with *salt, pepper* and *a bay-leaf* and let it stew in water just to cover for about 1½ hours. But stop before the meat begins to break up. Now add 100g (4 *oz*) *black pudding* and 100g (4 *oz*) *fresh mushrooms*. Taste it to see if there is enough salt and pepper and adjust this. Now fill the pastry-lined pudding basin, sealing the pastry over the top of the meat.

Tie two thicknesses of greased foil or greased greaseproof paper firmly over the top of the basin. The foil or paper should be pleated in the middle to leave room for the pudding to rise a bit.

Keep the left-over gravy from the stew pan and thicken it to your own requirements. Put the pudding basin in a pan, standing on an upturned saucer (this stops the basin cracking) with *boiling* water to come half-way up. Let it boil for 2 hours with a lid on, replacing the water as it evaporates with more boiling water.

Serve the pudding with freshly mashed and buttered potatoes, peas and turnips (swede turnips).

Basso Profundo

Newcastle must be one of the draughtiest corners of England, but they have very warm hearts to make up for the weather. The butcher calls you 'pet', everyone is pleased to see you and there is a marvellous street market along the quay on Sunday mornings with people buying knickers, spare bicycle parts and fresh fish right on the edge of the water.

Owen Brannigan, the singer, was born near Newcastle and once wrote that his idea of the perfect meal was grilled herrings from North – or South – Shields. Then Pot Pie 'known elsewhere than in North East England as Steak and Kidney Pudding. A Pot Pie Supper in Newcastle's Pen and Palette Club would be a night to remember in the life of the most fastidious gourmet!'

Yorkshire Cobbler

The beef-eating north of England is very partial to stews and casseroles. They can be very good if cooked properly and are sometimes served with home-made Lancashire muffins hot from the oven.

Yorkshire Cobbler has a kind of dumpling topping. Dice about 800*g* (2 *lb*) *stewing beef*, roll it in seasoned flour. Peel and chop about 200*g* (8 *oz*) *onions*. Fry both in 50*g* (2 *oz*) *beef dripping*. Drain and put the meat and onions in a casserole with 375–500*ml* (¾–1 *pt*) *stock*. Add 2 *bay-leaves* and *a little parsley*. Bake with a lid on in a moderate oven 180°C (350°F) Gas Mark 4 for 3 hours.

FOR THE TOPPING sift 150*g* (6 *oz*) *self-raising flour* into a basin, rub in 50*g* (2 *oz*) *butter* and add *milk* to make a soft but not sticky dough. Divide the dough into 8 pieces and roll these into balls on a floured board. Brush them with milk and put them carefully on top of the stew 20 minutes before it is cooked. Leave off the lid, and increase the oven heat to very hot 230°C (450°F) Gas Mark 8.

Alice's Rich Beef Pie

This used to be a hot favourite in Lancashire works canteens. The secret lies in including a piece of cow-heel which makes a gorgeous rich dark rib-sticking gravy that sets in a jelly when cold. This is grand with chips, either hot or cold.

Cut up 300*g* (12 *oz*) *shin beef* and put it in a pan with *an onion stuck with cloves* and *half a cow-heel*, dressed – you get it from a local tripe dresser, or some family butchers. Add *salt and pepper* and pour 500*ml* (1 *pt*) *brown stock* over it. This should cover the meat. Let it simmer for about 3 hours on top of the stove or in a casserole in the oven. Lift out the beef and cow-heel, strip off the meat and cut it in neat pieces. Pile it all into a shallow round pie dish. Add a little of the cooking liquor thickened if liked with a teaspoon of cornflour mixed to a paste with a tablespoon of water. Cover the pie with about 200*g* (8 *oz*) *savoury rough puff pastry*, brushing this with *milk or beaten egg*.

Bake the pie in a fairly hot oven 190°C (375°F) Gas Mark 5 for about 45 minutes until the pastry is golden. Make some gravy with the remaining cooking liquor and serve the pie with a cup of gravy, mashed potatoes and greens.

Rump Steak and Onions

A great favourite in the North Country, where some men still enjoy a nice underdone rump steak and onions for breakfast, with a cup of tea to go with it.

You need some *very tender rump steak* – about 4cm ($1\frac{1}{2}$ in) thick, well hung, marbled with fat and weighing 400g (1 lb) or more. It will be expensive and should come from a very good butcher or it will not be worth eating. Trim it if necessary, brush it over with *oil* and set it aside.

Peel 5 *or* 6 *onions.* Cut them in thin slices (I wear sunglasses for this and weep less). Heat some dripping in a frying-pan. Add all the onions at once, covering them with a lid or an old plate. Fry them gently for 5 to 6 minutes on a low heat, stirring occasionally. Take them off the heat. Add *salt, pepper* and *a pinch of sugar.* Drain off any surplus fat. Stir them up with a fork, go on cooking them for about 5 minutes until they are just tender. If they are wanted crisp do this part without the lid. If they are wanted soft and melting, leave it on except at the very end.

Start the steak after the onions have begun to cook. Grill it 6–7 minutes per side. Exactly how long depends, I'm afraid, on the thickness of the meat, the heat of your grill and whether you like the steak blue, rare, medium or well done. Get the grill really hot before you start. When cooked arrange it on the onions with knobs of butter over it. Serve it at once.

Salted Dry-Fried Steaks

Some Lancashire cooks do the steaks in a hot frying-pan with salt. They do not use the grill. It is a sort of dry-frying really. It fills the kitchen with black steak-flavoured smoke but the result is delicious. Put a thick white layer of salt all over the pan bottom. Get it really hot. Then add the steak. The salt stops the meat sticking to the pan and burning. Sear the meat in the pan 2 minutes per side, then a bit longer depending on how well you like it done. Then just wipe any surplus salt off and eat it.

Beef Sausages

In Lancashire and some parts of Yorkshire they make long thin beef sausages. They are darker than pork sausages, and some are flavoured with tomato. I do not myself like them quite so well as coarse-cut pure pork sausages but they are justly popular served with Yorkshire pudding.

They should be pricked and baked with a very little beef dripping in a tin in a hot oven 200°C (400°F) Gas Mark 6 for a good 20 minutes. The Yorkshire pudding, or the Savoury pudding, is done in another tin at the same time, with hot beef dripping.

Beef sausages are very good when pricked and fried with beef dripping until very crisp, then eaten with red lentils and bacon. Sprinkle a little salt on the bottom of the frying-pan, especially when frying sausages – it stops fat from splashing the stove. Sausage fat is often poured over the red lentils for added flavour, as for red lentils and bacon (see page 52).

Panakelty

Panakelty (or Panacklty or Panhackelty – everyone spells it differently) has been a great dish in the north-east for generations. It is basically a stew but some make it with sausages, some with left-over meat, and it used to be made with corned beef when this was cheap, and was also a good way of using up the Sunday joint. It is popular on washing day when mum is busy and it was a mainstay of the Jarrow marchers. Some Geordies say it gets its name because everything goes higgledy-piggledy into a pan.

Fry *two medium onions* gently in a little lard or dripping, put them on the bottom of an oven-proof dish, add 200*g* (8 *oz*) *corned beef or cold meat* left over from the roast, then some *carrots* in a layer and any *left-over cooked vegetables.* Finally add 2 *or* 3 *diced cooked potatoes,* with *salt and pepper* to your taste. Pour in 500*ml* (1 *pt*) *hot stock* (or hot *water* and *a stock cube*). Bake it in a moderate oven 180°C (350°F) Gas Mark 4 for about an hour. One miner's son from Castleton near Sunderland, who is a student in London, told me that he cooks the panakelty in a pressure-cooker. He puts in a layer of potatoes, then meat, and a layer of carrots and a layer of onions, then 250ml (½ pt) of stock. The carrots are cut in large equal pieces so they don't cook too fast.

'You'd be surprised how soon the vegetables are done in a pressure-cooker,' he said. 'And I put in ketchup though it is probably not correct.' The result is quite good but very different from most people's idea of the dish. But, like scouse, both the recipes and what people expect to eat with the label Panakelty on it vary widely.

Mrs Dorothy McCabe now of Brighton in Sussex, but who was born and brought up in Newcastle, spells it Panackalty and makes it with sausages. This is a very old North Country recipe, as she wrote to me. 'My grandmother, also my mother used it and I now carry on the tradition as my husband and friends love it. Have 4 *large raw potatoes*, sliced 12mm (½ in) thick. Lay them in a fire-proof dish, alternating with 400*g* (1 *lb*) *sausages* and 2 *large sliced onions*. Sprinkle these with *sage, pepper and salt*. Add enough cold water to cover. Put on a lid, bake it in a fairly hot oven 190°C (375°F) Gas Mark 5 for 30 minutes.

'This makes a delicious savoury and economical dish for lunch or an evening meal and gives a generous helping for four persons. If a second vegetable is required serve boiled buttered cabbage. No gravy is necessary.'

Dripping Toast and Chip Butties

Ever tasted a chip butty? It's a real scouse speciality, popular all over Lancashire and Cheshire. In my childhood it was just two penn'orth of chips sandwiched fresh and hot between two slices of bread and dripping. Though you would need a good deal more pence now. Especially delicious in cold weather, though as you get older your digestion won't really stand it.

Dripping toast is another North Country favourite, with

strong brown tea the spoon will almost stand up in. You save the dripping from beef and pork roasts, or even chicken dripping, and spread it thick on bread butties, or let it melt into hot toast. Indeed, freshly-made crisp toast spread thickly with bacon dip and served, quick and hot, for tea on a misty afternoon, is a dish for the gods. Thick salty beef dripping, all meaty from the roast, is delicious on hot toast too, and when creamed with thin English mustard is very good indeed in underdone beef sandwiches.

A classic English sandwich loaf, whether white or brown, and not too thinly sliced, is more suitable for toast – probably a British invention – than other kinds of bread, whether fine textured or crusty. Very good toast can also be made by spreading the hot toasted bread thickly with butter, then with sugar mixed with powdered cinnamon. This kind of toast should be cut in thin elegant fingers.

III
Pork

Christmas Pork and Chicken
Cumberland Sausages
Black Puddings
White Puddings
Ham, Gammon and Boiled Bacon
Bacon Saucers
Bacon and Egg 'Pie' or Tart
Red Lentils and Bacon
Red Lentil Soup
Bacon and Cow-Heel Pudding
Pease Pudding and Boiled Ham
Yorkshire Savoury Pudding
Haslet or Aislet
Savoury Ducks
Annie Funnell's Scratching Pie
Northumberland Ham and Leek Pasty

Pork

On the Cheshire–Shropshire border a lot of people have roast pork and chicken for their Christmas dinner. The two go well together and the custom goes back for centuries. The leg of pork is stuffed with sage and onion, the chicken is stuffed in the crop with a conventional parsley and lemon stuffing, and it is served with pork gravy poured over it. Egg sauce, roast potatoes, curled bacon and sausages are served too.

People put lighted Christmas trees, all done up in spangles, in the parlour window at Christmastime up there, to shine through the lace curtains for everyone to see. There used also to be side after side of bacon in the grocers' shops, hung in rows and done up in thin white knitted 'cheese-cloth' covers – like fat blondes in tights! As for the pork, the best crackling comes from joints with a good thick layer of fat underneath it. At the OLD THREE PIGEONS at Nesscliffe in Shropshire, the landlord feeds – or used to feed – his pigs on a daily ration of waste bread swilled down with a quart of beer. The beer gives the pork a slightly darker colour and a sweeter taste. It is not a very large sty, however, just enough pigs for the pub and, when there is not quite enough bread, the pigs get some rolled barley added.

Christmas Pork and Chicken

Rub the pork crackling well with salt before cooking to make it crisp, and place the leg on a grid in the baking tin. This is so the under-crackling does not fry in the dripping and become hard.

Allow 25 minutes per 400g (1 lb) and 25 minutes over in a

fairly hot oven 190°C (375°F) Gas Mark 5. If the meat weighs less than 1.25kg (3 lb) allow 40 minutes over. After dishing the pork, pour the surplus fat gently out of the roasting tin. Add a little water to the remaining juices and, if liked, some Worcestershire Sauce. Let it boil rapidly, stirring over a fierce heat until the liquid is somewhat reduced. This makes a good thin gravy. The chicken should be roasted for 20 minutes per 400g (1 lb) at the same temperature and well basted.

Cumberland Sausages

These, typically, are very good pure pork sausages and are often made and sold in one long piece without being divided into links.

Here is a farmhouse recipe for Cumberland Pork Sausages extracted from RECIPES OF LAKELAND.

'Mince 4½ lb lean pork, not too finely, add 1½ lb fat pork, ½ oz powdered sage, I pinch of marjoram, 1 oz white pepper, 3 oz salt. (Note, *no* bread.) Mix well. Test the flavour by cooking a little in a frying-pan, and add herbs and seasoning accordingly. Fill the casings and twist into links. These sausages will keep for weeks if hung on hooks on the ceiling.'

Most electric mixers now have, or can be fitted with, a sausage-making attachment.

Black Puddings

My own home county, Cheshire – wet, dank and full of cheese – is also celebrated for its short fat Black Puddings. These are superb for breakfast, whether with bacon or big hot fried Staffordshire oatcakes, like large floppy muffins as big as a frying-pan (see page 123). You get them fresh from the baker, then next morning cook them in bacon dip and have them with a fried egg and a piece of Black Pudding on top.

TO GRILL BLACK PUDDINGS Slash them here and there with a knife, or cut them into convenient lengths before grilling for about 4 minutes on either side and serving them, if liked, with grilled bacon or thick gammon rashers.

Black Puddings may also be heated through in hot water and served with mashed potatoes. You can also slice and fry them in dripping. Those made in the north-west of England are especially good and the Bury pudding, a thick plump pudding turned back on itself to look something like a large kidney, is a speciality of Lancashire and Cheshire. One sees them hanging in bunches from the ceiling in the better type of old-fashioned pork butchers' shops, looking like bunches of huge grapes.

They were much enjoyed by both yeomanry and gentry in Victorian England. Grilled Black Puddings still appear as a sort of savoury relish in the early morning after the Tarporley Hunt Club's annual dinner. This is held in the first week of November, at the end of the cubbing season and start of fox hunting, at the Swan Hotel in Tarporley, Cheshire, where the club has its own wines, plate and linen. Members dine in their own Hunt Room, the panelled walls of which are lined with about twenty life-sized portraits, in hunting 'pink', of former Presidents, about half of whom were MFHs (or Masters of the Cheshire Hunt) though the club calls them Managers. It was founded in 1762 and is limited to forty members, all of them men, so that I have not myself attended a dinner. I have always been told however that the members wear green knee breeches and green silk stockings beneath their pink coats, and that devilled bones and mulled ale are served with the grilled Black Puddings.

Black Puddings or *boudins* are as popular in France and Belgium as they are in the north of England, usually delicious and often served grilled with apple purée and buttery mashed potato. In some places in France they are eaten, traditionally, when people return from Midnight Mass on Christmas Eve.

In one small northern French town they have an annual *boudin* festival and contest with entries from all over

Europe, including about fifty from Britain. Prizes are awarded to the champion *boudin* maker.

People usually *buy* their Black Puddings nowadays in Britain, as in France. They are mostly excellent though a few do have an added black-pudding-dye to ensure 'an attractive dark finish'. On farms Black Puddings are often made in a dripping tin like faggots and savoury ducks. This is less trouble for the farmer's wife than filling sausage skins.

Black Pudding cut in chunks is very tasty in a steak and kidney pie and also in a hot-pot or a tatie pot. In Northumberland a hot boiled suet roll stuffed with leeks is often served with boiled Black Puddings.

White Puddings

White Puddings were made in Northumberland farmhouses in the nineteenth century at pig-killing time. The lights, hearts, brains and odd pieces of pork (what French charcutiers call the *couennes*) were minced and mixed with pearl barley, seasoning and what not, and packed into sausage skins. In Scotland they are usually called mealie puddings.

Ham, Gammon and Boiled Bacon

In Yorkshire some add a teacup of vinegar and half a dozen cloves to every 4.5 litres (1 gallon) of water for boiling a ham. Others add 2 tablespoons of black treacle to the water in which the ham is boiled. A ham to be eaten cold should be allowed to cool in the water in which it was cooked. Ham stock makes very good lentil soup, or pea soup when mixed with left-over pease pudding.

TRADITIONAL YORKSHIRE MUSTARD SAUCE to eat with cold ham is made by mixing 2 *parts dry mustard* with 8 *parts caster sugar* and adding *vinegar* to mix it. This must be made at least 24 hours before it is used.

Bacon Saucers

You will want four 15cm (6 in) pie plates. Melt *a little butter* in each and put 4 *rashers of streaky bacon*, without the rinds, in each. Put them in a moderate oven 180°C (350°F) Gas Mark 4. When the fat is smoking hot, pour in the batter, bake the batter till puffed up and golden and eat from the pie plates, hot from the oven. They are pleasant with ketchup.

FOR THE BATTER sift 100*g* (4 *oz*) *plain flour* and *a pinch of salt* into a basin. Make a hollow in the middle, add *an egg* beaten up in 125*ml* (¼ *pt*) *milk*. Beat this to make a smooth thick batter, and pour into the saucers.

Bacon and Egg 'Pie' or Tart Mark I

Bacon and Egg 'Pies', or Tarts, are made all over Yorkshire, but the methods vary. In some districts the pie is covered with pastry, in others left open, some people leave the eggs whole, others beat them with milk and then get the filling to cook like a custard. These, I think, are the best.

Line a 20cm (8 in) baking tin with fairly thinly rolled *shortcrust pastry*, sprinkling it with *pepper and salt.* Beat up 3 *large eggs* and with enough *milk* to bring the mixture up to 250ml (½ pt). Cut 2 *or* 3 *streaky bacon rashers* in small pieces, scatter them on the pastry, pour the egg mixture over it and sprinkle it with *chopped parsley.*

Bake the pie in a hot oven 200°C (400°F) Gas Mark 6 until set and browned. Sometimes a pastry 'lid' is put on the pie before it is cooked, but it then becomes a little stodgy, for my taste at any rate.

BACON AND EGG PIE Mark II

This is made by lining a dripping tin with shortcrust pastry. Cover the bottom with minced raw ham or bacon. Make a 'delve' or hollow in the ham for each egg so they stay in place. Break an egg into each hollow (4–6 should be used). Season well, cover the pie with a pastry crust. Brush with milk. Bake it in a moderate oven 180°C (350°F) Gas Mark 4 until browned and set. It is cut into squares when cold, and good for packed lunches – though the Mark I pie is, to me, the better of the two. Sometimes the whole eggs are pricked so the yolks run evenly through the pie.

Red Lentils and Bacon

A much-loved North Country dish, hot, filling and easy to cook, but no one seems to have heard of it down South.

There are two kinds of lentils: the ordinary red, or Egyptian, lentil that when cooked goes into a lovely mush within about ten minutes, especially if it has not been soaked first, and the much bigger brown, or German, lentil used with game in foreign casserole dishes. This keeps its shape however long you cook it. If lentils are unavailable, use previously soaked split peas in such recipes – red and brown lentils are *not* interchangeable.

FOR RED LENTILS AND BACON, boil 200*g* (8 *oz*) *red lentils* in unsalted water for 30 minutes without previous soaking. When cooked, strain them, add *salt and pepper* and 200*g* (8 *oz*) *hot fried through-cut bacon rashers.* Pour the bacon dripping into the lentils. Some cooks add tomato sausages.

Red Lentil Soup

In small hotels up and down the country the Farmers' Ordinary was where they served hot dinners to farmers on market days – boiled beef, carrots, dumplings with four other vegetables, or perhaps a cut off the joint. With jam roly-poly, or apple pie and cheese to follow. It was full of steaming leggings, gossip and pipe tobacco, competition was fierce and in those days you could often get a good sound meal well cooked on the premises, before they were overcome by frozen scampi and the gastronomic experience.

Red Lentil Soup was a great standby, it is made with the so-called Egyptian or red lentil, sold in most old-fashioned grocers' shops, not with the brown continental lentil used for foreign stews and salads.

Heat 2 *tablespoons good dripping* and in it fry 1 *peeled chopped carrot*, 1 *peeled sliced onion* and *a small peeled chopped turnip* (swede turnip). When the vegetables are just golden add 175*g* (7 *oz*) *red lentils* and fry gently, stirring for about a minute longer. Add 1 *litre* (2 *pt*) *stock*, 3 *or* 4 *bacon rinds, a ham bone* or some *bacon bones or* 2 *pig's feet*, from the butcher or pork butcher. Add *pepper, mixed herbs*, very little *salt* and bring it to the boil.

Let the soup simmer, chunnering away quietly to itself for about an hour – or until the lentils are cooked to a mush. Now purée them in the electric mixer with the pieces of vegetable. Put them back in the pan with their liquor and any meat or bacon scraps. Add 250*ml* (½ *pt*) *milk* and reheat it. Taste it for seasoning, it may need more salt. It looks nice sprinkled with chopped parsley.

Bacon and Cow-Heel Pudding

This is an old Lancashire favourite that is really a pie rather than a pudding. You want *a dressed cow-heel* from the tripe shop. Put it in a large pan, add *an onion stuck with* 3 *cloves* and 500*ml* (1 *pt*) *brown stock* – or enough brown stock to cover the cow-heel and onion. Bring it to the boil, then let it simmer for 3 hours. Cut the meat off the cow-heel, chopping it in neat pieces. Wrap these in about 300*g* (12 *oz*) *bacon rashers*. Put them in a 1 litre (2 pt) pie dish, add the *stock*, and a pie funnel and top it with *shortcrust pastry*. Brush the top with milk. Bake the pie in a moderate oven 180°C (350°F) Gas Mark 4 for about an hour. Dutton's Meat Stout used to be very popular with it.

Pease Pudding and Boiled Ham

In Northumberland, Pease Pudding is eaten with roasts, with sausages, with white puddings, even with sandwiches, with all kinds of pork cuts and with ham and boiled bacon. 'A grand tea we had, boiled ham, Pease Pudding and pickles,' they say locally. Boiled Ham and Pease Pudding has been an essential part of any celebration of standing in the North East, from weddings, christenings and funerals to New Year's Day parties, for longer than anyone can remember. No one knows when the two dishes came together, but Pease Pudding itself is a very very old dish which pre-dates the potato by centuries. There are various recipes for Pease Pudding and it can also be bought ready-made from the butcher. You see huge white enamel basins holding about 20kg (50 lb) of delicious freshly-made Pease Pudding in the butchers' shops but it soon goes.

Wash 200*g* (8 *oz*) *split yellow peas*, put them in a basin with boiling water to cover, add a *pinch of bicarbonate of soda* and leave them overnight. Tie them loosely in a cloth to leave room for the peas to swell.

Put them in a pan of boiling unsalted water and simmer for 1½–2 hours. Drain them well and mash them or rub them through a sieve. Add 50 *g* (2 *oz*) *butter or melted dripping*, some *salt and pepper*, and, if liked, 1 *large egg*. Pack them into a greased oven-proof dish or into a basin which is greased and lined with *brown breadcrumbs*. Bake in a moderate oven 180°C (350°F) Gas Mark 4 for 45 minutes. When cooked let the pudding shrink well, and cut it in pieces if done in a tin, or if in a basin, turn it out on a plate.

Yorkshire Savoury Pudding

I lunched at the HARE AND HOUNDS in Stutton village on Old Ale and some very good beef sandwiches, with pieces of onion, salty beef dripping and jellied gravy from the roasting tin inside them. Doreen Longden, the licensee, also gives you very small hot roast potatoes to eat in your fingers – much better than crisps. 'I bought a sack of those very tiny potatoes,' she said. 'I do them in the potato machine, then bake them in the roasting tin with pepper, onions and ordinary dripping.' They're champion! The pub is hidden away at the back of the village near the road to Pontefract and people come from all over Yorkshire for her Sunday lunch, often with a choice of three different roasts and poached salmon and the Yorkshire pudding served as starters, just with gravy in the proper manner.

'Have you ever had Yorkshire pudding with golden syrup?' she says. 'It's gorgeous, but the pudding has to be cooked in butter.'

People still talk about the WARS OF THE ROSES in Yorkshire; the pub, which is near Tadcaster was once the HQ for some people fighting in a battle at nearby Towton, after which the beck behind the HARE AND HOUNDS flowed red with blood. This, they say, is why it is the only part of Yorkshire where the dog roses are speckled with red.

Mrs Longden later gave me her recipe for Yorkshire Savoury Pudding which, as she says, 'is usually served in Yorkshire with goose, pork and similar kinds of meat'. It is sometimes cut into squares and served hot before the meat with a good thick gravy.

Take a large mixing bowl. In it put 200*g* (8 *oz*) *soft white breadcrumbs*, 75*g* (3 *oz*) *shredded grated suet or margarine*, 2 *tablespoons oatmeal*, 1 *tablespoon plain flour*, ½ *tablespoon dried sage*, 2 *raw grated onions*, ¼ *tablespoon dried marjoram*.

Mix it all well with a wooden spoon. Stir in 1 *beaten egg*, 125*ml* (¼ *pt*) *milk*, ½ *tablespoon chopped parsley* and some *salt and pepper*. Mix all the ingredients together and pour them into a very hot Yorkshire Pudding tin with a good spoonful of smoking hot melted dripping in it. Bake it in a fairly hot oven 190°C (375°F) Gas Mark 5 until browned.

Haslet or Aislet

Some country butchers make very good Haslet, usually to their own recipe. Unlike faggots and savoury ducks it is usually made in a long roll and though very good hot can be sliced and eaten cold like a continental terrine. It might be made with pig's liver and melt, or pig's fry, liver and lights, or heart with pieces of fat pork. Cooks in the big houses used, a generation or so ago, to make it for Christmas.

Put 400*g* (1 *lb*) *pig's liver*, and 400*g* (1 *lb*) of *melt and* *kidney* in a pan with 200*g* (8 *oz*) *peeled chopped onions.* Cover with hot water, bring to the boil and poach, bubbling gently for 5 or 6 minutes. Take the ingredients out of the pan and mince them. Add 200*g* (8 *oz*) *fine white breadcrumbs,* 400*g* (1 *lb*) *sausage meat, salt and pepper,* about *a dozen finely-chopped fresh sage leaves* and *a little grated nutmeg.* Mix well and shape into a roll. Wrap in *a piece of leaf or caul fat.* First soak the caul in cold water, squeeze and pull out into a thin lacy piece. Put the caul-wrapped haslet in a greased baking tin. Bake it in a moderate oven 180°C (350°F) Gas Mark 4 for about 2 hours, reducing the heat if it is getting too brown. Leave the caul fat on top to become deliciously crisp.

Savoury Ducks

Rural Derbyshire is full of recipes no one seems to have heard of sixty miles away and some country bakers and butchers sell the sort of food your great-grandfather might have enjoyed. I do not know whether Mr Ted Hall's butchers' shop is still on the village green at Hartington, but when I visited it some years ago the window was full of handmade Stand Pies, Legs of Lamb skewered in the Caul (or flead fat), Pressed Hock and Savoury Ducks. These, as Mr Hall explained, are much the same as Faggots only the onion is put in raw, not boiled first, and the mixture is roasted whole in a tin. Then later it is cut in squares for sale, while Faggots are made in small pieces.

All the same, some country people make Savoury Ducks with potatoes, pig's liver and onions more like a Tatie Pot. Haslet, or Aislet, is another similar thing but made in one long roll, like a meat roll and it can be sliced in rounds.

Chop 200*g* (8 *oz*) *onions* and 50*g* (2 *oz*) *streaky bacon* with 400*g* (1 *lb*) *pig's liver.* Add 200*g* (8 *oz*) *soaked bread* squeezed dry. Mix well, adding 1 *tablespoon chopped fresh sage, salt, pepper* and 1 *egg.* Melt some lard in a roasting tin, put in the mixture. Bake it in a moderate oven 180°C (350°F) Gas Mark 4 for a little over an hour.

Annie Funnell's Scratching Pie

Scratchings are (of course) the crisp little pieces of fat or crackling left after the pig's flair fat has been melted down for lard and dripping; these are called scruggins on the Welsh border but scratchings in the Midlands. When made crisp in the oven and rolled in salt they go well with drinks and aperitifs and should be rescued from obscurity. This pie is a first cousin to Fitchett Pie and the sweet rum and mutton pies made in Cumberland at Christmas. The recipe was sent to me by Mrs M. Betchley of Steyning in Sussex.

'Line a deep round tin with *shortcrust pastry.* Sprinkle 100*g* (4 *oz*) *scratchings* over the bottom. Mix together 100*g* (4 *oz*) *pig's liver,* 200*g* (8 *oz*) *pig's heart* (*parboiled*), 200 *g* (8 *oz*) *pig's tongue* (*parboiled*). Add 1 *teaspoon mixed herbs, salt, pepper,* 1 *teacup soft brown breadcrumbs,* 1 *teaspoon brown sugar, a pinch of caraway seeds* and *a handful of currants.* Spread this over the scratchings. Break 2 *eggs* over it, pricking the egg yolks so they spread over the egg white, but do not mix yolks and whites together. Cover this with 1 *boiled sliced onion* and *another* 100*g* (4 *oz*) *scratchings.* Moisten the mixture with *stock,* not with onion water. Finally put on a shortcrust pastry lid. Bake in a moderate oven 180°C (350°F) Gas Mark 4 for approximately 45 minutes.'

Northumberland Ham and Leek Pasty

Northumberland is a district of brass bands and Giant-Leek-Shows where people win huge prizes, a trip to America or something like that. They go in for The Fattest Leek or the Longest Leek competitions and some of the thin leeks are two metres (seven feet) tall; they nourish them on all sorts of things ... Everybody goes in for it and you can see the most amazing leeks growing in almost every cottage garden from Aukland to Amble. When it gets towards competition time some of the growers stand guard over them night and day for fear of their precious leeks being stolen.

The leeks that do not win are sometimes made into boiled leek puddings to eat, hot and steaming, with a cold joint or with some of the excellent local black puddings. They also make a very good leek pasty, delicious for a picnic or to take to the races. This old North Country dish is not really so different from the much better known French *flamiche* or *tarte aux poireaux*, or even the fashionable *quiche lorraine* now so popular in London.

Chop 400 *g* (1 *lb*) *well-washed leeks* in chunks. Pour boiling water on them. Leave them for 5 minutes, then drain them thoroughly. Line a well-greased Swiss roll tin with *shortcrust pastry*. Chop 200*g* (8 *oz*) *ham or boiled bacon*, sprinkle it over the pastry, adding the chopped leeks.

Beat 2 *large eggs* with *salt, pepper* and 4 *tablespoons milk*. Pour it over the meat and vegetables. Cover the top with pastry, damping the edges and pinching them together to seal it. Brush the top with egg or milk so it will be brown when cooked. Bake it first in a hot oven 200°C (400°F) Gas Mark 6 for 20 minutes, then reduce the heat to very moderate 170°C (325°F) Gas Mark 3 and allow plenty of time for the pastry to cook through.

IV
Meat of All Sorts

Crokky Pies and Pail Dinners
To Roast an Old Hen in Dripping
Lancashire Hot-Pot
Pickled Red Cabbage
Mutton Saucer Pies
Shepherd's Pie
Tatie Pot with Black Puddings
Tripe
Tripe with Parsley
Tripe and Ham Pie
Tripe and Sausages
Grouse
Roast Yorkshire Grouse
To Roast a Hen
Coaching Days
Boiled Rabbit Smothered in Onions
Mother's Rabbit Sandwiches
Farmhouse Game Pie
Roast Venison Done in Foil

Meat of All Sorts

As a child I lived near the Trent and Mersey Canal. You could get to it easily past Davenham Church and over the River Dane jogging along in the pony and trap. You saw the horses going along the towpath and there were hump-backed brick-built bridges with stone parapets. From a distance the low long canal boats, often with a man and his dog at the helm, seemed to be gliding through the fields, for the canal was built high over the salty marshes with steep grassy embankments. If you were a child you could not see the water until you were quite close.

The canal children often had lovely thick jam and treacle butties but sometimes it was just bread and dip, which I think is best of all. This is just slices of bread fried in bacon fat or simply dipped into it and then used to wipe the pan around, and eaten while the dip is still warm.

If the boatman or his wife let you go inside you saw a painted cabin hung from ceiling to floor with fancy plates and you always smelled the dinner cooking, often all in one go in a pan or bucket. Roly-poly pudding, potatoes, vegetables and bacon done in one pot to save space and fuel.

Crokky Pies and Pail Dinners

It is not a bad idea! You can cook some boiled potatoes during the last half hour in the pan with your roly-poly pudding (which is quite all right when properly wrapped, as it must be, before cooking), and even with a piece of bacon – allowing about 30 minutes per 400g (1 lb) and soaking it first overnight in cold water.

I like parsley sauce and cabbage with it, but this must be done separately. A Crokky Pie is one cooked in a crock, or pudding basin, in a pan besides the vegetables. It is often topped with suet pastry and two thicknesses of greaseproof paper tied on firmly with string. Sometimes it was a big steaming pan with a rabbit hidden under the vegetables. Boatmen often set snares or went with a dog into the canal-side coverts after rabbits for the pot. I have never poached a pheasant, but rabbits are easy to catch on summer afternoons, with a good dog, since they lie up sleeping in the long grass tussocks all over the fields. Another little girl and I used to catch them with an Irish terrier. When the dog has caught one of course you have to pounce, get the rabbit by the ears and pop it into a shopping basket.

To Roast an Old Hen in Dripping

It was a lock-keeper's wife on the River Weaver who told me, years later, how to do this. First stuff the bird. Then put 400g (1 lb) of dripping in a large pan. Put an old saucer in the bottom with a grid on top of it. Get the fat smoking hot. Then put the hen on the grid just above the fat. Cover the pan with greaseproof paper or foil and put the lid on tightly with a weight on top. Leave it to cook over a moderate heat for 3 hours. The old hen will be golden brown and can be served as roast chicken. A useful recipe if one does not have an oven.

Lancashire Hot-Pot

Like all casserole dishes the Hot-Pot will wait in the oven for hours without becoming dry or spoiled. I remember once talking to a circus troupe who told me that they used to begin cooking the Hot-Pot in their caravan oven as usual, then they wrapped it in several layers of newspaper and a blanket and took it to bed with them to act not only as a hot-water bottle but to finish cooking gently in the warmth under the eiderdown.

Get the butcher to chop the meat, *600g (1½ lb) altogether lamb chops and scrag end*. Roll it in *flour, salt and pepper*. Warm a heavy iron casserole or a proper round hot-pot dish. Put *a tablespoon of dripping* in the bottom. Roll it around to grease the inside. Lay the meat in it. Put *two or three large peeled and roughly-sliced onions* on the meat. Peel *two large potatoes* and slice them in rounds about 6mm (¼ in) thick. Lay them on the onions. Then cut 2 *or* 3 *more large potatoes* in halves. Put them on top to make a crust, sprinkle them with a *very little flour*. Put some *seasoning* in the cracks between them. Pour in enough *hot stock* or water to cover the sliced potatoes and just touch the halved ones. Put a lid on it. Bake it for about 4 hours in a very moderate oven 170°C (325°F) Gas Mark 3 or longer if liked. Remove the lid towards the end to brown the top.

Pickled Red Cabbage

This is a 'must' with Lancashire Hot-Pot. Cut *a firm, dark, red cabbage* in shreds. Put layers of cabbage and *salt* alternately in a basin, the last layer should be salt. Next day drain and rinse the cabbage, pack it loosely into jars and cover it with cold *spiced vinegar*.

SPICED VINEGAR can be made quickly as follows: put the vinegar and spices in a basin and to each litre (2 pt) of vinegar allow *6g (¼ oz) whole cloves, 6g (¼ oz) cinnamon stick, 6g (¼ oz) blades of mace, 6g (¼ oz) allspice berries and a few peppercorns.* They are best tied in a muslin bag. Cover all this with a plate then stand the basin in a pan with cold water to reach half-way up. Bring the water in the pan slowly to the boil. Take the pan off the heat. Let it stand for a good two hours then strain the vinegar and it is ready to use. Pour it into the jars of prepared red cabbage and screw down the tops but without letting any metal come in contact with the vinegar. The cabbage is ready in about a week.

Mutton Saucer Pies

Butter or grease some saucers and line them with *shortcrust pastry*. Fill them with a mixture of *minced mutton or lamb, salt, pepper, a little chopped parsley* and *fresh thyme*, 1 *small finely-chopped onion* and 2 *large mushrooms chopped*. Moisten with *a little stock or milk*. Cover each with a round of pastry, brush the top with milk. Bake them in a moderate oven 180°C (350°F) Gas Mark 4 for about 45 minutes.

Shepherd's Pie

Shepherd's 'Pie' itself may well have originated on the Cumberland sheep farms – like the excellent but now very rare mutton hams – as a way of making the best use of tough mutton. Shepherd's Pie is excellent, too, when made with venison instead of mutton. Cheap forequarter cuts are quite good enough. It is, of course, known as COTTAGE pie, not SHEPHERD'S pie, when made with minced beef. In some pubs they now serve it in individual pie dishes, with a thick layer of grated cheese over the mashed potato. This becomes deliciously brown and crunchy in the oven.

They have a unique breed of hill, or fell, sheep – the Herdwick – in the Lake District which survive blizzards and snowdrifts better than other breeds. People say that centuries of tough living on the three thousand foot high fells have taught the sheep to anticipate snowfalls a full day before even the weather men get drift of them. If they do get caught in a snowdrift, it is said they can live for a couple of weeks by eating their own fleece. They were called Herdwick after the huge sheep runs established by the monks at Furness Abbey.

This unusual Shepherd's Pie, from Mrs Birkett of Cumberland, has layers of vegetable over the mince and under the mashed potatoes. It is extracted from *Farmhouse Fare* (a collection of recipes from country readers published by the *Farmer's Weekly*).

Mince some *cold meat*, put it in a roasting tin with a *sliced onion, pepper, salt,* and *half a teacup of water*. Then add a layer of *sliced cooked carrots*, a layer of *sliced cooked turnips* (turnip swedes) and a layer of *sliced cooked par-*

snips. Now a layer of *peas*. Cover the whole thing with *mashed potatoes*, mark them with a fork and bake it in a brisk oven 190°C (375°F) Gas Mark 5 until the potatoes are nicely browned.

Tatie Pot with Black Puddings

Cut 300*g* (12 *oz*) *middle neck of mutton or lamb* in nice pieces and put them in the bottom of an oven-proof dish or hot-pot dish in layers with 1 *sliced black pudding*, 2 *large peeled sliced onions* and 1 *peeled diced carrot*. The vegetables are really best laid on top of the meat. Add *salt and pepper*. Peel and slice 600*g* (1½ *lb*) *potatoes* and cover the meat and vegetables with them. Pour in about 375*ml* (¾ *pt*) *water*, to come not quite to the top of the potatoes. Put a lid on the dish or pot.

Put it in a very hot oven 230°C (450°F) Gas Mark 8 for 30 minutes then reduce the heat to moderate 180°C (350°F) Gas Mark 4 and let it cook for about 2 hours or more, taking off the lid during the last 40 minutes so the potatoes get brown and crunchy.

This is a famous farmhouse dish, once popular in Lakeland pubs. Tatie Pot suppers used to be popular local events, and were often made for Shepherd's Meets, local Dales Shows, Hunt Meetings and the like. It makes a perfect supper in the public bars of some country pubs after a wet day on the fells and an evening drinking.

In Northumberland a Tatie Pot is usually made with bacon pieces (bought cheaply from the grocer) onion, potatoes and stock.

Tripe

Tripe, liver, kidneys, sweetbreads and pig's feet all go very well with a bottle of red wine. Most of us thoroughly enjoy these things in little restaurants abroad when they are a 'speciality' of the house – but don't a lot of the others turn their noses up at the same dishes here when they get home?

Tripe has been well-loved in the north of England for generations and is usually beautifully cooked, though there are some who sniff at it as 'down market' or old-fashioned. Yet there is a superb tripe dish in Lyon – people travel miles (kilometres) for it! And another in Marseille which hums with garlic. Tripe is the great gastronomic speciality of Lisbon in Portugal and the famous *tripe à la mode de Caen* is so very much enjoyed by the French that they have a World Tripe Contest every year in Caen, with entries from all over France to find the best cooked dish. There is no prize money but to win one of the precious diplomas can set a Frenchman up in catering for life. *Tripe à la mode* is a delicious creation, simmered for hours in cider and Calvados, with herbs and onions.

But in how many three-star hotels in the north of England, I wonder, would you get a good dish of tripe and onions? It used to be served in the old-fashioned tripe parlours, often with mashed potatoes. Now almost vanished, these tripe parlours were favourite resorts on Market Day. Here are three very old family recipes.

Tripe with Parsley

This version is from Mrs J. Arden, of East Didsbury, near Manchester, who says: 'Buy 200*g* (8 *oz*) *of dressed tripe* and then cook it till very tender, cutting it in small pieces. Butter a pie dish. Sprinkle a layer of *soft white breadcrumbs* and *chopped parsley* on the bottom. Add a layer of tripe, *salt and pepper.* Add a little more parsley and crumbs, then another layer of tripe, salt and pepper, and sprinkle it with the rest of the breadcrumbs, 6 heaped tablespoons in all. Beat up 2 *eggs* with 250*ml* (½ *pt*) *milk.* Pour this over the tripe and crumbs. Put 25*g* (1 *oz*) *butter* on top in small pieces. Bake it in a moderate oven 180°C (350°F) Gas Mark 4 for 20 minutes until the custard is set.'

Tripe and Ham Pie

'This is an old family recipe. It is difficult to put exact quantities down, as so many can be varied depending on the larder and the family,' as Mrs R. W. Mercer, of Woolton in Liverpool, wrote to me. 'Put *thinly-sliced cold boiled ham* – *or raw ham* – in the bottom of a pie dish. Then a layer of *cooked tripe* with its jelly adhering. Season it with *pepper* but not much *salt* as the ham is salty. Add a little *butter* and fill the dish in layers in this manner. Put in a few tablespoons of *good brown gravy*, then cover the dish with *puff pastry* and brush it with *milk*. Bake it first in a hot oven 200°C (400°F) Gas Mark 6 to set the pastry. Then reduce the heat to moderate 180°C (350°F) Gas Mark 4 to finish cooking it 1–2 hours. Cover the pastry with a piece of greaseproof paper, or foil, if it seems to be getting too brown.'

Tripe and Sausages

Stew 400*g* (1 *lb*) tripe and 2 *large peeled chopped Spanish onions* gently in salted water. When they are tender drain off the water, add 200*g* (8 *oz*) *coarse well-spiced country pork sausages*, pricking them and laying them on top of the tripe. Add *milk* just to cover and let it all simmer on a low heat until the sausages are tender. It is served with mustard and mashed potatoes.

Grouse

A brace of grouse from the Yorkshire moors and some well-blued farmhouse Wensleydale cheese was the classic gift from nineteenth-century country cousins hoping to be invited to Belgrave Square, or somewhere in Mayfair, for the London season.

Cold roast grouse is particularly delicate when very underdone and served with a watercress salad – a most enjoyable picnic dish for Doncaster races. Very tough old grouse (which is all most of us can hope to afford nowadays) can be cut up and put in a steak and kidney pie. They give it a sort of *je ne sais quoi*, especially when well hung.

ROAST YORKSHIRE GROUSE

A recipe from Anton Mosimann of the Dorchester Hotel, London. He is their young *maître chef des cuisines.*

For four people, draw and pluck 4 *grouse*, leaving the fine feathers on the legs. Put *a sprig of rosemary* inside each bird and *a thin piece of pork fat* on the breast of each. Truss them. Season and roast the birds for about 18 minutes in a very hot oven 220°F (425°F) Gas Mark 7. Prepare and then toast 4 *slices of French bread*. Spread them with *pâté* (see below for *farce au gratin*). When the grouse are cooked remove the rosemary, the pork fat and the string. Serve the birds dressed on the *croûtons*, topped with *beurre noisette*, and replace the pork fat. Garnish them with game chips and picked watercress. Serve roast gravy, bread sauce, and breadcrumbs (browned under the grill) separately.

FOR FARCE AU GRATIN Sauté 15*g* ($\frac{1}{2}$ *oz*) *shallots*. Season 25*g* (1 *oz*) *chicken liver*, 25*g* (1 *oz*) *grouse liver*, and add them to the shallots, cooking them lightly so the livers stay pink. Add a touch of *brandy* and pass them through a sieve with 25*g* (1 *oz*) *cooked mushrooms* and a good 25*g* (1 *oz*) *pork fat*. Season.

To Roast a Hen

In my childhood in Cheshire there were always numerous old laying hens or boiling fowls to be cooked as best one might. In those days most people first boiled and then browned them in the oven, but this is how we cooked them at home – in one of those steel kitchen ranges with flues and dampers. I believe that, whatever the oven, the method may well owe something to Mademoiselle, the French governess who arrived from somewhere near the Franco-Swiss frontier when I was six or seven, and that it was similar to that used on farms in eastern France.

Put *a lump of butter* and *a bunch of parsley*, some *salt and pepper* inside the bird. Cover the top and sides with *bacon rashers* and put the *hen* in the roasting tin in not more than 2.5 cm (1 in) depth of *stock* (water and a chicken cube). Add the *giblets*, some *fresh herbs* and the *juice of a large lemon*. Cover the whole roasting tin completely with greaseproof paper, or foil. Bake it in a slow oven 150°C (300°F) Gas Mark 2 for a good 3 hours, basting it from time to time. The bird turned brown all over and was served with forcemeat balls, thick chicken gravy, some jacket potatoes and, sometimes, Yorkshire pudding.

Coaching Days

The building of the turnpike roads and the coming of proper mail-coach services was the making of all kinds of people. Samuel Smith's, of Tadcaster, the oldest brewery in Yorkshire, where they still make real ale – traditional beer in wooden casks – first flourished in the days of the old stage- and mail-coaches, for Tadcaster was one of the stages or posts where the coachmen changed horses on the road – between York and the north.

Regular stage-coach travel between London and York began in 1703. The coaches set out on Mondays, Wednesdays and Saturdays, travelling between the BLACK SWAN in Holborn (London) and the BLACK SWAN in Coney Street, York. One of the stops, or posts, where they changed horses was the BELL INN, Stilton, Huntingdonshire. The passengers used to buy the local raised pork pies and ripe blue cheese to eat on the journey. They soon became famous. The cheese came to be called Stilton and is thought to have been invented by a farmer's wife, Mrs Paulet, who lived just south of Melton Mowbray and was the publican's sister-in-law. The pies came from Melton Mowbray too.

Of course there can have been nothing like thundering down the old turnpike roads on the top of a stage-coach at the end of December for giving you an appetite. The outside passengers, wrapped in heavy capes and fustian coats, their feet muffled in straw, used to tell funny stories and talk about food to keep out the cold. It may, or may not, surprise the reader to learn that I have never actually travelled by stage-coach, but all the same I do agree with William Hazlitt the essayist, when he wrote that there is nothing quite so good as a nice dish of Boiled Rabbit Smothered in Onions after a wet and wintry journey: 'What a delicate speculation it is, after drinking whole goblets of tea, the cups that cheer but not inebriate, and letting the fumes ascend into the brain, to sit considering what we shall have for supper. Eggs and a rasher, a rabbit smothered in onions, or an excellent veal cutlet?' he wrote. 'And how fine it is to enter some old town, walled and turreted just at the approach of nightfall, or to come to some straggling village, with the lights streaming through the surrounding gloom, and then, after inquiring for the best entertainment that the place can afford, to take one's ease at an inn?'

The son of a dissenting minister, Hazlitt was brought up in the North West like myself, a district where you need plenty of good hot food: three eggs and inch-thick gammon rashers (none of your thin London stuff) flanked by hot Bury puddings, to keep out the cold and damp. So come in and have a bit of rabbit before the damp gets into your very bones.

BOILED RABBIT SMOTHERED IN ONIONS

It makes no difference whether it is one of those tender rabbits bred for the table or a cut-up frozen one from Australia or China.

Soak the *pieces of rabbit* in cold salted water for a good hour. Put them in a pan with very hot water to cover, adding *seasoning*. Then when it boils reduce the heat and let it simmer for nearly two hours. That's all. Serve it with plain boiled potatoes and the *rich onion sauce* poured over it.

FOR THE ONION SAUCE mince 300*g* (2 *lb*) *peeled onions* and stew them gently in *butter* over a low heat with a lid on the pan so they 'melt' rather than brown. After removing the rabbit boil the stock down violently until it only comes to about 375ml ($\frac{3}{4}$ pt) and is full of rich rabbity flavour.

Stir this into the onion purée adding seasoning to your taste. Lastly stir in some hot thick *cream* – then pour the sauce over the rabbit and surround it with the mealy boiled potatoes. In William Hazlitt's day they used sometimes to leave the rabbit whole, stuff it with forcemeat, sew it up and boil it, then have it with caper sauce and it was served dished up on a nice clean-tasting spinach purée.

Mother's Rabbit Sandwiches

'We lived in the Rugby House at Hall Road, between Southport and Liverpool in the 1930s and had an old black cat called William (the Conqueror!) who used to catch rabbits but never ate them. He would kill them, bring them home, and lay them at my mother's feet. Skinned, jointed, then popped into a heavy black casserole with a knuckle of ham costing about 6d, whole small onions and carrots, plenty of pepper and always cloves, they were slowly cooked in the oven (a coal range) and later made into a pie for Saturday night's supper.' Mrs Vera Jones, of Blackpool in Lancashire, continued – 'Remains were made into sandwiches for club members on Sunday afternoon, who adored my mother's "game" sandwiches. Many elderly Rugby Union players will have fond memories of them. She did have a regular order for rabbits with the local poultrymonger, as William's supply was apt to be erratic. My mother and William have been dead many years and I'm now a grandmother myself, but I still love rabbit.'

Farmhouse Game Pie

Line a pie dish with *shortcrust pastry* and arrange the *meat left from a roast grouse or partridge* on it with a *small onion* minced and browned in *butter*, 100g (4 *oz*) *thinly-sliced mushrooms* and 3 *grilled roughly-chopped bacon rashers* – in layers. Cover them with a gravy made from boiling the carcass with carrots, etc. Add a lid of pastry and brush with beaten egg. Bake it in a hot oven 200°C (400°F) Gas Mark 6 for 35 minutes. This can be eaten hot or cold cut into wedge-shaped slices.

Roast Venison Done in Foil

Venison is lean dry meat, best roasted in foil – this replaces the old huff pastes of Victorian England. Red deer needs longer cooking than roe deer which is more tender.

It is as well to leave the *haunch of venison* in a marinade, or pickle, for 24 hours before roasting. Put it in a pot with 1 *sliced carrot*, 1 *peeled sliced onion*, some *salt*, 12 *crushed peppercorns*, 2 *bay-leaves*, some *mixed herbs*, a piece of *chopped garlic*. Add *a teacup of oil* and about 250 *ml* (½*pt*) *red wine*. Turn the meat from time to time in the marinade. Take it out before roasting, wipe it, smear it thick all over with dripping. Wrap it in greaseproof paper. Then enclose it completely in foil like a parcel.

Roast it in a moderate oven 180°C (350°F) Gas Mark 4 for 20 minutes per 400g (pound). About 30 minutes before it is done take off the coverings. Sprinkle the meat with a little flour, baste it well, let it brown. Use the marinade to make a gravy for it. Hot jacket potatoes may conveniently be served, as well as Cumberland Sauce.

If you would like your name put on the venison list for a whole carcass of fallow, red or roe deer, write to: The Estate Office, New Holker Estate Co. Ltd, Cark-in-Cartmel, Grange over Sands, Cumbria. As they become available the Estate Office will telephone and make arrangements for you to collect it on a cash-and-carry basis.

Sizes and weights vary widely according to whether it is red, roe, or fallow deer and whether it is a doe or a buck – from about 40–80kg (100–200 lb) for a red stag to 8–12kg (20–30 lb) for a roe doe. The herds in the great deer park of Holker Hall, Cark-in-Cartmel are culled annually, being killed humanely with one shot through the neck. This is really the picking out of surplus deer so the herd does not get too big for its feeding ground.

V
Brawn and the Like

Beef Brawn
Cow-Heel
Lancashire Beef and Cow-Heel Tart
Jellied Bacon and Cow-Heel
Harvest Brawn
Oxtail Brawn or Shape
Pea Wack and Brawn
Pestle
Old-fashioned Souse
Yorkshire Potted Oxtail

Brawn and the Like

Brawn used to be the mainstay of Edwardian country house breakfasts, along with game pie and devilled pheasant. It is still beautifully made in the North of England, where it is a great speciality. People go in for lovely Brawn Suppers and in my childhood it was the sort of thing one used to have at farmhouse teas with great doorsteps of warm newly baked bread with an inch of butter on them and that kind of strong, brackish tea in which a spoon is said to stand upright. But nobody seems to make it Down South nowadays, probably because the commercial brawn you get in London and places is frequently so awful, with unmentionable scraps of meat embedded in uniform pink jelly. Yet a well made brawn can be just as good as the most exquisite coarse farmhouse pâté or the famous Austrian *schweinssulze*, which is served in thin elegant slices with finely chopped onion and vinegar on it.

Beef Brawn

In some of the dales of the West Riding of Yorkshire they make excellent tongue and ox-cheek brawn, which is turned out to serve. It looks most elegant on the cold table, is very good with salad, and may be sliced and served instead of pâté for 'starters'.

Put 800*g* (2 *lb*) *ox-cheek*, 1 *pickled* (*salt*) *ox-tongue* and 1 *split dressed cow-heel* in a very large pan with cold water to cover the meat, but no salt. Add 1 *roughly-chopped onion*, 1 *stick of celery* (if available), 2 *chopped carrots* and 1 *chopped parsnip*. Bring it to the boil then simmer gently until the meat is tender. Chop the meat, throw away any bones, place it in basins. Strain the liquor over it and leave to set.

Cow-Heel

Cow-heel, which always seems more determinedly gelatinous than calves' feet, is a favourite in the cattle market towns of the north of England. Some say there is nothing like half a cow-heel added to soup stock for giving it a good tacky rib-sticking quality, and a lot of people in Lancashire will tell you that 50g or 75g (2 oz or 3 oz) of cow-heel is invaluable for stews and so on, adding 'body' and making the liquor more gelatinous. If you have not been brought up there, perhaps it might, at first, seem a bit of an acquired taste, like the delicious *pieds et paquets* of Marseille, fried cuttlefish, or any other regional delicacy. It is well worth trying.

LANCASHIRE BEEF AND COW-HEEL TART though very good hot, is even better cold, as it goes all jellied and slices nicely. It is excellent for picnics and packed lunches, and used to go into working men's bait baskets.

Jellied Bacon and Cow-Heel

Jellied Bacon and Cow-heel used to be popular for Wakes Week, eaten with thick slices of new bread and butter and mixed pickles.

Put a *piece of boiling bacon* in a pan of cold water and bring it to the boil. Throw this water away, then cover it once more with cold water, adding *a dressed cow-heel*, split if possible. Add 12 *peppercorns* tied in a bit of muslin. Let the whole thing simmer. When tender, take out the bones, chop the cow-heel and the bacon, having removed any skin. Pack it in a basin, fill up with stock. Let it set. This is served sliced.

Harvest Brawn

The brawn, set in a pudding basin with hard-boiled eggs, is the sort of thing one used to have at farmhouse tea years ago with great doorsteps of warm newly-baked bread with half an inch of butter on them, two kinds of home-made jam, fresh scones, Cut and Come Again Cake, and that kind of strong sweet tea in which they say a spoon will stand upright.

Cut up *a big rabbit* and put it in a basin of cold salted water for several hours to soak. This whitens the flesh. Meanwhile, simmer *a couple of pig's trotters*, split lengthways by the butcher, in a pan of water for about 2½ hours. Add the rabbit, 12 *peppercorns*, 3 *cloves* and *a piece of mace*. Let it simmer for another couple of hours, in a casserole in the oven if you like. The meat should be dropping off the bones, then cut both pork and rabbit in chunks. Rinse out a large pudding basin with cold water, decorate the bottom with *a sliced hard-boiled egg*, then put in the pieces of meat. Strain the stock over them through a fine sieve. Leave it to set, then turn it out on a dish. Chicken – preferably a boiling fowl or half of one – can be used instead of rabbit.

Oxtail Brawn or Shape

A very good picnic dish. Simmer *an oxtail*, with *a slice of ham* and 2 *cloves*, in 750*ml* (1½ *pts*) *water* for 3 hours. Take the meat off the bones, discard the cloves. Chop the meat finely, adding a *teaspoon salt*, ½ *teaspoon pepper* and ½ *teaspoon freshly-grated nutmeg*. Pour the strained liquor over it and leave it to set. Turn it out to serve.

Pea Wack and Brawn

'We always made our own brawn with half a pig's head, or as we call it here in Liverpool, a pig's cheek,' says Mrs Mary Van Eker of Bramberton Road in Walton, Liverpool. 'You cannot get them very much now. They were sold very cheap and the eye was removed by the butcher. The poker was put in the fire and when red hot the face was singed all over. Then it was boiled for about two hours. It was lifted out of the pot to cool. The meat would fall away from the bone. It would be chopped up in cubes and put into a basin.

'A cup of boiling stock would be poured into the basin to cover all the meat and then a plate upsidedown was placed on the top of the basin and the brawn was allowed to cool and set. As you said, a pig makes its own jelly. It was delicious.

'The stock was not wasted. It was used for making pea soup. Pea Wack, we called it. Lentils or split peas and carrots and onions were thrown into it. That's where we get the name whackers from. We never wasted anything.'

Pestle

My enthusiasm for pig's trotters (something I buy boiled, egged and crumbed in France hoping to bring them home and have them grilled for supper) is shared by Mrs Rita Vale, of Seaburn in Sunderland, who wrote to me in 1977 to say that for many years her mother used to make a delicious brawn with them.

'If you do try it, I hope that you will enjoy it as much as we all have done. In Lancashire, where I was born, it is called Pestle.' Now although I come from nearby Cheshire I did not know that in Lancashire this kind of brawn is called Pestle. I generally make mine with *half a pig's head*, but this recipe is delicious too, and very cheap. Mrs Vale's mother 'used 1 *or* 2 *trotters* with the fore shank if possible, as it has more meat on it than a hind'. Put them in a pan with seasoning and then cover them with cold water. Bring them to the boil and then skim them. Let them simmer gently for a few hours, or until the meat falls off the bones. Strain the liquor into a basin, adding more seasoning if necessary. Remove all the bones and chop the rest of it very finely with an old-fashioned chopper. Then put it into the strained liquor stirring well. 'This sets beautifully, is easy to cut, tasty, and what's more, economical. I still make it.'

Old-fashioned Souse

Sousing usually means cooking in a mixture of water and vinegar, or in wine, perhaps with spices – hence the expression 'soused' or 'pickled' for someone who has been drinking.

'It is delicious eaten with pickles, mustard, piccalilli or red cabbage. This is one of my grandmother's recipes, and I still make it,' as Mrs E. King, of Hexthorpe, near Doncaster, wrote to me some years ago about souse.

'Cut up 400*g* (1 *lb*) *shin beef* and 1 *dressed cow-heel*. Put them in a large stew pan, cover them with water. Bring to the boil on the stove, then put into the oven to simmer gently. Simmer until all the cow-heel has left the bone and the meat is tender. Pour off the liquid into a basin, mash all the meat, etc., with a fork, then pour in the liquid. Season with *salt and pepper*. Mix well, then pour into basins and leave to set overnight.'

Yorkshire Potted Oxtail

This is different from the brawn or shape, being more like a pâté or potted hough. It is delicious with hot buttered toast.

Put *two oxtails*, cut in pieces, in a basin of warm water. Leave them about an hour to soak. Then put them in a stew jar or basin with 500*ml* (1 *pt*) *water*. Stand this jar or basin in a pan of water, or put it in a slow oven 150°C (300°F) Gas Mark 2 standing in a roasting tin with hot water to come half-way up the jar or basin. Let it simmer gently for 6 hours until the fat falls off the bones. Add *seasoning*. Strain the liquor from the oxtail pieces. Bone and then mince the meat. When it is nearly cold add the liquor, taste for seasoning. Pour it into little potting pots. When set, pour *melted* *butter* over the top of them to seal the meat from the air. It keeps for a week or so in the refrigerator, and is a most useful party or teatime dish for those with a solid fuel cooker.

VI
Cheese Dishes

To Pot Cheshire Cheese
Lancashire Cheese
Cheese, Bacon and Onion Pie
To Make Cream Cheese
Cheese Scones
Derbyshire Cheese
Cheese and Onion Pie
Wensleydale Cheese
Pan Haggerty

Cheese Dishes

Farmhouse cheese was made from the milk of cows owned by the farmer making the cheese, and sometimes by neighbouring farmers too. All the cattle grazed on exactly the same soil, in the same climate and on similar grass which gave these particular cheeses an individual flavour. In creameries the milk comes in from various farms and is mixed. The difference is similar to that of wine from a single chateau, or even village, compared to a blend of wines from a large area. 'Cheese-making has become big business and is seldom done in the farmhouse today, largely because of the demand for liquid milk and the regulations concerning the production and sale of farmhouse cheese,' as they write in *Farmhouse Fare* (1973 edition), a book of recipes from country housewives collected by *Farmer's Weekly*. 'But this does not mean that some of these old recipes cannot still be used today if you have a house-cow or, for some reason, a quantity of milk is unexpectedly available. Some of the small soft and lactic acid cheeses are still in demand in high class shops or on local market stalls.'

Cheshire is the oldest English cheese, crumbly rather than flaky, and unlike Cheddar it is not imitated abroad. About fifty years ago there was an annual output of about 18,000 tonnes (20,000 tons) of farmhouse Cheshire but the real thing is getting rare now and blue Cheshire, the epicure's dream, a lovely thing with a natural blue mould, is now made on only one or two farms in Shropshire and Cheshire. One can sometimes buy them in Nantwich market in Cheshire on Thursdays and Saturdays. Occasionally there is a little farmhouse Cheshire that has 'gone a bit wrong' – crumbly, at bargain prices. One can mix it with herbs and make potted cheese of it.

There is a firm just over the border in Shropshire which

sends good blue Cheshire cheese by post and real farmhouse Cheshire cheese too. The farm producing it lies within a mile of their premises so that they always get the cheese in the finest condition, but of course the postage, which is included in the price, is appalling, almost killing the postal trade for many rural craftsmen. At the moment of writing it costs:

Blue Cheshire	– 800 g	(2 lb)	£2.78
	– 2kg	(5 lb)	£6.06
	– 4kg	(10 lb)	£10.93
Farmhouse Cheshire	– 800g	(2 lb)	£2.43
	– 2kg	(5 lb)	£5.19
	– 4kg	(10 lb)	£9.18

This includes postage and packing.

To Pot Cheshire Cheese

'I have a cook book with the date 1780, by Mrs Ann Partridge, of George Street. It is very hard to read because it is in very old print. There are some recipes in handwriting and here is one for potting Cheshire cheese.

' "3 *lb Cheshire cheese* pounded in a mortar with ½ *lb fresh* (*unsalted*) *butter* and *a gill rich white wine*, 9½ *oz mace* finely beaten. When all is well mixed press it hard down in pots and cover it with clarified butter. Keep it cold." Please excuse writing as my hands are bad, my age is 74.'

This is from Mrs Elizabeth A. Wilkinson of Dormas Wills Est, Southall. Fresh butter means unsalted butter and in those days a gill was often half, not a quarter, of a pint. One should add it little by little till the right creamy texture is obtained.

Lancashire Cheese

Fifty years ago Lancashire cheese was made in the Fylde, mainly along the shores of the Irish sea, in farm kitchens there, and it ripened on shelves near the range. It is still made in about five farmhouse kitchens mostly near the

Cheshire border. Almost all is eaten locally; it is rarely sold in the south though a few years ago, at any rate, you could still buy 'spoiled' Lancashire cheese, cheap but crumbly, in Nantwich market in Cheshire on Thursdays. Lancashire Leigh Toaster cheese, made near the village of that name, is famous and like Red Leicester it makes superb Welsh Rarebit, soft enough to spread, it melts easily, toasts well and is one of the best cheeses for cooking. A white cheese that is a mixture of two days' milk, matured for a fortnight, milled, salted and pressed, it becomes slightly acid when aged for three months.

Cheese, Bacon and Onion Pie

'My mother used to make this when we were children,' said Mrs L. Barnes, of Bolton in Lancashire, in a letter to me. 'Chop 100*g* (4 *oz*) *bacon* without the rind in small pieces. Chop 1 *small onion* and 100*g* (4 *oz*) Lancashire cheese finely. Put it all in a pan with *a knob of butter* and *a little milk*. Bring it to the boil, stirring, and simmer for a few minutes. Line a buttered pie dish with *shortcrust pastry*. Pour in the cheese mixture, sprinkle with grated cheese. Bake in a fairly hot oven 190°C (375°F) Gas Mark 5 for 15–20 minutes.'

To Make Cream Cheese

'Put *one large spoonful of steep*[1] to *five quarts of afterings*,[2] break it down light, put it upon a cloth on a sieve bottom, and let it run till dry, break it out and turn it in a clean cloth. Then put it into the sieve again, and put on it a two pound weight, sprinkle a little *salt* on it and let it stand all night, then lay it on a board to dry. When dry lay a few strawberry leaves on it, and ripen it between two pewter dishes in a warm place, turn it and put on fresh leaves every day.'

From *The Experienced English Housekeeper* by

[1] Steep is rennet.
[2] Afterings is skimmed milk.

Elizabeth Raffald, Manchester 1789. I have added some full stops because Mrs Raffald wrote the recipe as one sentence.

Cheese Scones

These are very popular in Northumberland. Sift 200*g* (8 *oz*) *self-raising flour* with ½ *teaspoon dry mustard* and ½ *teaspoon salt* into a basin, then rub in 50*g* (2 *oz*) *lard*, adding 125*g* (5 *oz*) *grated cheese*. Mix it with *a beaten egg* and a very little water; do not get it too wet. Roll it out on a floured board until about 6mm (¼ in) thick. Cut it out with a scone cutter or the top of a sherry glass. Bake the scones in a hot oven 200°C (400°F) Gas Mark 6 until well risen.

Derbyshire Cheese

This is a very old cheese, though not made on farms now. In the nineteenth century the opening of the LMS Railway provided a new outlet for the farmers' milk, taking it away to big centres and cities so that Derbyshire cheese became very rare. Then in 1869 a local creamery was opened and Derbyshire cheese reappeared. It is a pleasant hard but mild cheese that suffers a little from being rather like Cheddar. Years ago they used also to make a special sage cheese at midsummer for sale at the Christmas Cheese Fairs in Derby and Bakewell. This was a blue-veined cheese with a bunch of sage leaves in the middle that flavoured the whole cheese (much as caraway seeds flavour a French Munster) but the practice must have died out. A generation ago people who had lived in the North West all their lives had neither seen nor heard of it, now it is quite common but has changed a lot. In recent times they have minced the sage and mixed it with spinach juice which, though it adds nothing much to the flavour, gives the cheese a dramatic green stripe through the middle. Later some creameries went in for a brilliant green and orange marbled effect.

Cheese and Onion Pie

Kedleston Hall, Lord Scarsdale's seat, has belonged to his ancestors since the thirteenth century. The present eighteenth-century house is designed partly by Matthew Brettingham Senior, and partly by Robert Adam. It is a huge Palladian villa in stone in the very grand manner, some of it inspired by the Pantheon in Rome. Amazingly, the servants' pavilion and kitchens and the family pavilion were built about half a mile apart, which must have made good cooking difficult.

From the cook at Kedleston Hall in Derbeyshire who wrote to me 'I have been a cook all my life and am still working,' Mrs Constance Bevan told me. 'I was formerly cook to Sir Bernard Docker and made country dishes for him. I am now working for Lady Scarsdale at Kedleston Hall. I was born in the north country and we were always cooking and baking bread and pies. This pie, which is very tasty, is an old north country one. It is called Cheese and Onion Pie.

'Mix 200*g* (8 *oz*) *self-raising flour* with ½ *teaspoon salt*, 100*g* (4 *oz*) *butter* and 100*g* (4 *oz*) *pure lard*. Mix this to a soft dough with 2 or 3 tablespoons of water. Flour it and roll it out and line a pie plate with the pastry.

'Then grate 2 *large peeled onions* and 200*g* (8 *oz*) *strong cheese* on to it. Season a small quantity of *thick fresh cream* with *salt and pepper*. Whip it lightly and spread it over the mixture. Cover it with pastry and flute the edges securely. Brush the pastry with milk and bake the pie in a fairly hot oven 190°C (375°F) Gas Mark 5 for 30–35 minutes.'

Wensleydale Cheese

The dale heads of Yorkshire, South Durham and the Lake District are famous for their Wensleydale cheese but it is now all made in creameries, except perhaps for a very little farmhouse Wensleydale made for the use of the farmer and a few close friends.

'The only great English *bleu* that can compare with Stilton,' writes my old friend M. Pierre Androuet, famous Parisian *maître fromagiste.* 'Smaller in size, available unaged and then called Wensleydale White. But Stilton is the best of the English cheese to my taste.'

Wensleydale cheese should be uniformly blue-veined with a rough coat, for a smooth one is a sign of a hard harsh interior, and it should have a rich creamy texture soft enough to spread, with a lovely aftertaste.

It is sometimes eaten with cold Christmas pudding and port, or with a slice of plum cake. It is said to have been made originally from sheep's milk (like Roquefort) by the monks at Jervaulx Abbey. Nowadays it is made, secularly, of cow's milk.

Pan Haggerty

Do not confuse Panakalty with the Pan Haggerty they have for high tea and supper round Newcastle. This is, I suppose, what a chef would call a *gratin* of potatoes and onion and it is very good, whether or not you have fried eggs with it.

Peel and slice 400*g* (1 *lb*) *potatoes* and 200*g* (8 *oz*) *onions* very thinly. Dry them in a cloth. Heat 1 *tablespoon of dripping* in a big thick frying-pan, put in the onions and potatoes with 100*g* (4 *oz*) *grated cheese* in layers, seasoning each layer with *salt and pepper.* Fry it all gently until cooked then brown it under the grill.

VII
Sweet Puddings

Honeycomb Mould
Blackcurrant Fool
Brandy or Ginger Snaps
Cannon-Ball Pudding
Manx Junket
Wet Nellies
Prunes in Port
Ratafias or Macaroons
Ratafia Pudding with Wine Sauce
Skipton Pudding
Spotted Dog
Roly-Poly Pudding or Suety Jack
Old-fashioned Velvet Cream

Sweet Puddings

It was of course Mrs Dennett who taught me how to milk a cow. This was when I was a child in Davenham, Cheshire, and naturally we did it by hand. She herself was a sort of Noah's Ark figure in a green cricket cap (which hid her curlers), a long skirt, army boots and with a figure like a cottage loaf. I loved her very much.

She lived in a cottage just up the road. There were two cows and a pig, a whole party of loose-living hens, and a pair of geese of which I was terrified. We used to go mushrooming across the fields and in search of buried treasure. This was when I was about seven. Once, remarkably enough, we dug up a whole pirate's hoard under the raspberry canes – exactly where I'd always known it would be. There was an old pewter tobacco jar and a leather pouch stuffed (if I remember right) with pieces of After Eight.

We had honeycomb mould and thick warm bread and butter at tea-time to give us strength for milking. For this you wore a hat, sat on a three-legged stool with your head against the cow's tummy – and pulled. Well, you know perfectly well where, it's a kind of syncopated one-hand-after-the-other, like trying to rub your tummy and pat your head at the same time.

If a cow doesn't like you she won't let out any milk. Not only that – unlike a horse – she can kick forward under her stomach. 'Cow-up' I used to say. 'Cow-up there, cow-up' in my very deepest and firmest voice. Say 'cow-up' in any North Country meadow full of cattle about milking time and they all come running at you in a brisk gallop hoping eagerly for their tea.

Honeycomb Mould

To make the honeycomb mould we used to enjoy so much, heat up 500*ml* (1 *pt*) *milk* with the *grated rind of a lemon* and, if you like, *a bay-leaf* from the garden. Sprinkle 4 *level teaspoons of gelatine* into 4 *tablespoons of boiling water* and stir until it melts. Beat up 3 *egg yolks* with 75*g* (3 *oz*) *caster sugar*. Put them into the top of a double saucepan (with hot but not quite boiling water in the pan beneath). Stir in the warm milk and cook, stirring all the time, until it thickens enough to coat the back of a spoon. Take it off the heat and for heaven's sake don't let it boil as it would curdle at once and go lumpy like a sort of scrambled eggs. If you have no double pan use a basin standing in a bowl of simmering water. Add the melted gelatine, then gently mix or fold in the 3 *egg whites* whipped so stiffly the basin may be turned upsidedown without them falling out. Pour it into a 1 litre (2 pt) mould or basin rinsed with water. Put it on the cold dairy floor, or in the refrigerator, to set before turning it out.

In summer we often had this pretty pudding which separates into two parts, one frothy, the other lemony, garnished with raspberries or redcurrants from the back garden. Mrs Dennett rolled them in sugar, laid them round it and we sometimes had cream as well.

Not many people nowadays in urbanized England I suppose have been lucky enough to taste a large beaker of milk which has been milked straight into the mug from the cow the way I used to have it so often as a child. You get it all warm, smelling faintly of new-mown hay and with a deep frothy head on it like a glass of beer. It is most enjoyable. Children mostly get a milk moustache from drinking it.

Blackcurrant Fool

Country people in the Lake District make a very pleasing simple 'fool' by pressing 400*g* (1 *lb*) *stewed blackcurrants* through a sieve then stirring in the contents of *a tin of con-*

densed milk. As the milk is sweetened there is no need to add sugar, and the mixture will thicken to a good 'fool' consistency.

(From Underskiddaw Women's Institute.)

Brandy or Ginger Snaps

A great Yorkshire favourite, when filled with whipped cream they make a good ending to a dinner party and can accompany a good white dessert wine, even a most distinguished one, very pleasantly. They are rather fiddly to make but freeze well. Ormskirk Gingerbread is very similar. These things were once sold at fairs and under the hissing carbide lamps on market stalls. Some people still call them fairings.

For about 3 dozen fairings or brandy snaps: Put 100*g* (4 *oz*) *butter*, 100*g* (4 *oz*) *Demerara sugar* and 125*g* (5 *oz*) *golden syrup* in a pan and heat it gently, stirring, until the butter and sugar have melted. Sift 100*g* (4 *oz*) *plain flour* with 2 *teaspoons ground ginger*, add it to the melted sugar, etc. Beat it well until the mixture is smooth. Oil a baking tin lightly, and put 6 tablespoons of the mixture on it widely spaced to allow for spreading.

Keep the rest of it warm until ready to use it. Bake in the centre of a very moderate oven 170°C (325°F) Gas Mark 3 for 8 minutes or until they are pale golden. Leave them on the baking tray for 1 minute.

Then lift the brandy snaps off with a palette knife and roll each round the handle of a wooden spoon (several spoons or a long clean dowel rod will be needed) so that the smooth side of the brandy snap is outermost. Leave it for 2 minutes to set. Then slide the brandy snaps off and cool them on a wire rack. Repeat with the rest of the mixture.

To freeze brandy snaps: Pack them in a rigid polythene container carefully putting greaseproof paper or foil between the layers, cover the container, seal and freeze. To serve them, unwrap and thaw the brandy snaps at room temperature for 1 hour. Serve them plain or filled with whipped cream. In the air they soon lose their crispness, and if not to be eaten or frozen at once, should be kept in an airtight tin.

Cannon-Ball Pudding

This is very good served with hot golden syrup mixed with a little lemon juice. It only takes 30 minutes to cook. Mix 100*g* (4 *oz*) *soft white breadcrumbs*, 100*g* (4 *oz*) *flour*, 100*g* (4 *oz*) *moist brown sugar*, with 100*g* (4 *oz*) *shredded suet* and the *grated rind and strained juice of a lemon*. Add *a beaten egg* and make the mixture into small dumplings, pulling off the bits of pastry dough and rolling them round in floury hands. Drop them into a pan of boiling water. Boil them for about 30 minutes, gently. If there is a real rolling boil they will disintegrate. Heat some butter, pour this with more brown sugar over them, or simply pour warm golden syrup over the top. Cream is almost superfluous with them.

Manx Junket

This is called BINJEAN in the local Manx tongue and makes a delicious cold dish served with sugar and cream. Warm 500*ml* (1 *pt*) *milk* to blood heat (the milk must never boil nor have been boiled for it will not then make junket). Add some *sugar* and *a little freshly-grated nutmeg* – this will float on top and apart from the delicate flavour it looks charming. Then take off the heat and stir 1 *teaspoon rennet* – known locally as 'steep' – into the warm milk. Then pour the 'binjean' or junket into a pretty dish to set. Rennet is sold in bottles in most pharmacies and it keeps for a long time in the kitchen cupboard, though not for ever of course.

Wet Nellies

This is a Merseyside delicacy. It was popular during and after the last war. People tell you that when bakers and confectioners make sponge cakes and put them on trays in layers the jam and the wet part soak through, so the bottom layer is very soggy and jammy and you cannot sell it. This used to be given or sold off cheaply to the children who went round to bakers' and confectioners' shops asking for a pennorth of scraps. 'It is things you cannot sell that are given to kids' people say. Or 'wet Nellies are anything with a hot sticky filling – it could be Apple Charlotte, anything like that'. Some Liverpool people say that it is just any old sponge cake or fruit cake with Golden Syrup poured over it.

Prunes in Port

Not what Nanny recommended. The old-fashioned squashy dried prunes are used and they are soaked in port for several weeks until they have imbibed both the wine and the flavour. They are served with a good English egg custard, and too many prunes can make you distinctly tiddly.

Put 200*g* (8 *oz*) *dried prunes* into a glass jar, tight packed. Add *ruby port* almost to cover. Close the jar to prevent evaporation. They need not be cooked. Some people, however, soak dried prunes in cold tea, then simmer them in it when soft, adding several tablespoons of black treacle to the cooking liquor. Dried apricots soaked in old brown sherry are excellent too with a good syllabub or with whipped cream or an egg custard.

Ratafias or Macaroons

Atkinsons of Windermere is a small firm that began as a family grocery business making a few biscuits and sweets beside the shop in Ambleside seventy or eighty years ago. Though bigger now, they still have the same air of old-fashioned quality. I have found their things in high class grocers' shops all over the country – boxes of ratafias, the tiny macaroons which are one of the essentials of a proper Victorian trifle, Derwent toffee, rum-flavoured butter candy and the famous Kendal Mint Cakes. They also do Francis Lemann's Thin Captain Biscuits, which are not so dry as a water biscuit nor so soggy as a cream cracker: 'for over 200 years the premier cheese biscuit of the world' as it says on the tin, 'still as good as when first made in 1747'. Of course I have not myself been buying the Thin Captain Biscuits since 1747, but I do not expect they have changed much. Very good with Wensleydale cheese.

Ratafia Pudding with Wine Sauce

'Put enough water into a stewpan to come rather more than half as high as a 1.5 litre (3 pt) mould, of whatever shape you please, and put it on a low heat,' says Mrs Lila Jenkins, of Harworth in Doncaster, Yorkshire, in this recipe which she once sent to me. 'Remove the warmed mould and *butter* the inside well. Stick *stoned raisins* and *glacé cherries* on the butter to make it look ornamental. Arrange *ratafias* to cover the whole of the inside of the mould. Cut 6 *small sponge cakes* in half, and put them in, mixing a few ratafias and cherries among them; then put in more ratafias till the mould is about three parts full. Now whisk 7 *large eggs* lightly. Pour upon them 750*m* (1½ *pt*) *sweetened boiling milk.* Whisk well and pour into the mould. Tie a cloth over the mould or put a cover on and put this into the boiling water in the stewpan. It will take rather more than an hour to boil, turn it out on to a dish, pour wine over it and send some to the table in a sauce boat. It must be sent to the table as hot as possible and is served with Wine Sauce.'

WINE SAUCE Into a clean pan put 50*g* (2 *oz*) butter. Put it on the fire and when melted stir ½ *tablespoon flour* into it until it is quite smooth; mix by degrees with *a wineglassful water,* ½ *wineglass brandy* and 2 *wineglasses white wine,* with enough *moist sugar* to sweeten it; mix these together, put them on the fire, keep stirring it till thick (it ought not to boil) pour it into a sauce boat and send to the table.

Skipton Pudding

Make a baked custard from 4 *egg yolks, 500ml* (1 *pt*) *milk*, 2 *heaped tablespoons sugar*. Place this in the oven in a water bath. Top it with *ratafias*, then when cold with *marrow and pineapple jam*. Whip the 4 *egg whites* so stiff the basin may be turned upsidedown without them falling out. Fold them into 250 *ml* (½ *pt*) *whipped, sweetened cream*. Heap this over the jam and custard.

Spotted Dog

When did you last sink your teeth in a Spotted Dog? It is the kind of thing that elderly millionaires and rich gourmets, sated by too much expense-account living, long for but rarely get.

Sift 200*g* (8 *oz*) *plain flour:* with *a teaspoon of baking powder* and *a pinch of salt*. Add 100*g* (4 *oz*) *shredded suet* and enough water to make a dough you can roll out into a rectangular shape. Scatter 150*g* (6 *oz*) *dried fruit* – currants, raisins, sultanas, on it. Press them in lightly. Roll up the dough into a cylinder – like a Swiss roll. Butter some foil. Wrap the pudding in it completely, then in a floured cloth – a tea towel or kitchen cloth dipped in water and sprinkled with flour. Tie the ends tightly and tie it round the middle loosely to leave room for it to swell. Put it in a pan of boiling water. Let it boil for 2 hours, never stopping. Top it up with boiling water from a kettle when necessary. Unwrap and slice. Serve with brown sugar.

Roly-Poly Pudding or Suety Jack

This is made in the same way as Spotted Dog, only a little sugar is added to the dough. Then when it is rolled out it should be spread thick with plum jam or black treacle, instead of being garnished with dried fruit. Boil it up and cook it as before.

Old-fashioned Velvet Cream

Melt 8 *sheets of leaf gelatine* or 20g ($\frac{3}{4}$ *oz*) *powdered gelatine* in 125 *ml* ($\frac{1}{4}$ *pt*) *brown sherry* with 10 *lumps of sugar.* When cool strain it into 500*ml* (1 *pt*) *thick cream* and stir until it thickens. Pour into wetted glass custard cups. Serve when cold and set. It may be set in a wetted mould or china basin with ratafias placed round the edge.

VIII
Tarts

Bilberries
Bilberry Tart
Bilberry Pie
To Ice the Pie Crust
Bakewell 'Pudding'
Duke of Cambridge Tart
Little Lemon Curd Tarts
Old Middleham Tart
Moorland Tart
Treacle Tart
Breadcrumbs
Westmorland Threedecker
Wilfra Tarts
Yorkshire Cheesecakes or Curd Tarts
Curd for Tarts, with Vinegar
Shortcrust Pastry

Tarts

Tarts, or 'plate pies', are baked on tart plates in the north of England, not in the flan tins and flan rings used elsewhere for *quiche lorraine* and other continental delicacies. Flan tins have a lip round the edge, nearly 2.5cm (1 in) high, tart plates have none. The old tart plates were mostly enamelled or tinned metal, but nowadays ovenproof glass is often used. Some say the tart is not then so good, as the glass is too thick to let the heat through the pastry properly. When a baking tin with a lip round the edge is needed, people often use a square dripping tin in the North.

Delicious tarts are made all over the north of England, and in variety. Some are served with whipped cream spiced with rum and, in the Lake District, with rum butter. Some are associated with a village or a festival, some with both. Confusingly, some of them are called 'pies', or sometimes 'plate pies' because they are made in a pie plate, not a pie dish like a 'dish pie'. A Yorkshire 'stand pie', on the other hand, is one made with hot water crust pastry that will stand alone without benefit of pie dish. It is generally called a 'raised pie' in other parts of the country. There are many good English dishes without any real names attached to them and they are apt to be named puddings or pies, regardless.

After all, mince pies are not really pies but tartlets, and contain no mince, while a pudding may be anything from a steamed concoction with currants and sugar in it to a kind of sausage.

Bilberries

Bilberries are very much a regional delicacy, for although everyone likes them in Lancashire and Yorkshire, they say you can't sell fresh bilberries in the south of England – or even in Lincolnshire or over the border in Scotland. Amazing! I think they are delicious myself and remember munching them all raw and purple, rolled thick in sugar, as a child in Cheshire.

Bilberries make luscious dark purple Summer Puddings. Very small one-person bilberry tarts are also a speciality of the French Alps, when the fruit is ripe on the mountain slopes in July and August. One finds them in all the *patisseries* and little restaurants round Champéry. Yorkshire miners say there is nothing like a bilberry tart for taking down the pits, as they do not go mouldy in the coal mines like other fruit. One can get fresh bilberries in a few shops for about a week in southern England in late summer, and, of course, one can often buy quite nice bottled bilberries with a little of the fresh taste. American blueberries, however, are a different fruit altogether, larger and without that special smoky flavour. English bilberries are no bigger than currants and grow in ones and twos in small bushes on the moors and on some scrub-land. I have picked them in Cheshire and years ago people used to gather them in the West Riding with rakes, but now the bilberries mostly come from Poland.

Bilberries, in fact, are so well liked all over the north of England – right up to the Scottish border and down to the Midlands, and in Wales, anywhere that they used to grow wild – that the Poles have specially-chartered boats which put in regularly to Hull in July and August with over 10,000 baskets a week, when there is a good crop. But even the Polish bilberry boats are getting scarcer than they were, for the Poles are processing more and more of the fresh bilberries themselves. They freeze or bottle them now for export, instead of shipping them fresh.

Bilberry Tart

Butter a tart plate and line it with *shortcrust pastry*, crimping the edges with a fork. Fill it to within 2.5cm (1 in) of the edge with *bilberries* which have been picked over, rinsed in a little cold water and drained in a sieve. Add 2 *heaped tablespoons of sugar*. Arrange strips of pastry across the top in a trellis pattern, or top the tart with a pastry 'lid' if liked, and sprinkle with a little sugar before baking.

Bake the tart in a fairly hot oven 190°C (375°F) Gas Mark 5 for about 15 minutes. In Derbyshire a little chopped fresh garden mint is sometimes added to the pie.

Bilberry Pie

This one is made in Yorkshire and Derbyshire, in a pie dish, not on a tart plate. Pick over 600*g* (1½ *lb*) *bilberries* removing any leaves or little stalks. Butter the inside of the pie dish and put in the bilberries sprinkled with 150*g*–200*g* (6 *oz*–8 *oz*) *sugar*; add about 3 *tablespoons water* and a pie funnel. In Derbyshire a little chopped fresh mint is sometimes added to the pie for flavour. In Yorkshire, a pie made half of bilberries and half of peeled, cored cooking apples is popular. Cover the pie with *shortcrust pastry* and bake it in a moderate oven 180°C (350°F) Gas Mark 4 for about 45 minutes.

TO ICE THE PIE CRUST The pie crust can be iced in the ancient manner, but then less sugar is added to the fruit. If the pie is to be iced, take it out of the oven 10 minutes before it is done. Let it cool slightly. Spread royal icing thickly over the pie crust. Put it back in a rather cooler oven until the icing is very slightly browned on top. This is very good when the pie is made with sour fruit – damsons, gooseberries, rhubarb – as it makes a good contrast.

Alternatively – and if puff pastry is used – before the pie first goes into the oven, the raw pastry crust can be brushed with cold water and sprinkled very thickly with caster sugar. Press it in lightly. It browns the pastry and glazes it a little. Some pies are just sprinkled with sugar after they are baked, but then the crust should be brushed with milk before baking.

Bakewell 'Pudding'

Derbyshire people mostly say that the Bakewell Puddings are not what they were when they were young. 'It's the butter – or maybe the eggs,' some say. 'There ought to be two sorts of jam – raspberry and apricot – with flaky pastry . . . so rich you wouldn't believe it.'

It is still very delicious, however, and, of course, much finer and richer than that curious cake-like affair called a 'Bakewell *Tart*' in the south, a dish never mentioned in Derbyshire. There are several 'original' recipes, and other North Country puddings and pies which are clearly of the same family. I think, however, that we can settle for that of the Rutland Arms, in Bakewell, where they are said to have invented the original pudding a couple of hundred years back. It is also the hotel where Jane Austen stayed while writing *Pride and Prejudice*. Mr Oulsnam was chef at the Rutland Arms in 1955, and showed me the proper old oval pudding tins in which the Bakewell Pudding should be made. They have sloping sides as deep as your thumb, are about 15cm (6 in) across and look like a doll's hip bath.

Grease the Bakewell Pudding tin, line it with *flaky pastry* and leave it overnight. Cover the pastry next day with *raspberry jam*, then make the rich filling. For the filling: beat 8 *eggs* and 200*g* (8 *oz*) *sugar* together until they are pale and running off the whisk in ribbons.

Now, having melted 200*g* (8 *oz*) *best butter*, run it into the egg mixture. Beat it together before adding 100*g* (4 *oz*) *ground almonds*. Pour into the pastry case and bake in a hot oven 200°C (400°F) Gas Mark 6 until set.

Duke of Cambridge Tart

Line a 20cm (8 in) buttered tart plate with *shortcrust pastry* made from 150*g* (6 *oz*) *flour*, 75*g* (3 *oz*) *butter* with *a beaten egg* to moisten it. Melt 75*g* (3 *oz*) *butter* gently in a pan, stir in 75*g* (3 *oz*) *caster sugar*, and then the *yolks of* 2 *eggs*. Heat gently, stirring all the time, bringing the mixture almost to the boil. Stir in a good *large teaspoon of rum or brandy* and pour it into the pastry-lined tart plate. Brush the pastry edges with *egg white.* Bake in a moderately hot 190°C (375°F) Gas Mark 5 oven until it is golden brown.

It is to be eaten cold. Sometimes candied peel is sprinkled over the pastry before the egg mixture is poured in.

Little Lemon Curd Tarts

Home-made lemon curd tastes much better, more creamy, and yet more strongly of lemon than the manufactured kind, and is one of our best, though much neglected English specialities, virtually unknown abroad.

For little lemon curd tarts, butter some patty tins. Line them with *shortcrust pastry.* Prick the bottoms. Put *a spoonful of marmalade* in each. Add enough *lemon curd* to fill the pastry cases. Bake them in a moderate oven 180°C (350°F) Gas Mark 4 for 15–20 minutes.

This lemon curd recipe is from the Saddle Room in Hartington, Derbyshire, where they serve teas – with home-made jam and scones – in some converted loose boxes. Their cream is clotted in Matlock.

Beat up 225*g* (9 *oz*) *butter*, 800*g* (2 *lb*) *sugar*, and the strained *juice of* 6–7 *lemons.* They do not use the grated lemon rinds in Hartington, they say it keeps better without them. Heat the mixture gently until the sugar melts, either in a double saucepan or in a pan standing in a bigger one of hot water brought just to the boil. Stir 6 *lightly-beaten eggs* into the butter mixture. Heat, stirring all the time until it goes as thick as cream. Do not let it boil as the eggs will scramble. Cook it gently for two more minutes. Bottle in warm jars.

Old Middleham Tart

Roll out 150*g* (6 *oz*) *shortcrust pastry* to line a 23cm (9 in) tart plate. Trim the edges and use the trimmings to make a pastry lattice decoration for the top of the tart.

Mix 100*g* (4 *oz*) *desiccated coconut*, 100*g* (4 *oz*) *sultanas*, the *juice and grated rind of a lemon* and 100*g* (4 *oz*) *black treacle*. Warm the treacle slightly to make it easier to mix and pour it all on to the pastry. Roll out the trimmings, twist them, lay them across the filling in a lattice pattern. Bake in a fairly hot oven 190°C (375°F) Gas Mark 5 for about 30 minutes. This Yorkshire tart is very good hot but becomes pleasantly 'chewy' when cold.

Moorland Tart

They live well in rural Derbyshire, for they have everything: eggs and cream, meat, trout and grayling, plenty of game, and bilberries on the moors. They eat honey with lamb chops and the old people are – or were – very fond of crab suppers on Sunday night after prayer meeting, and there is a formidable beverage called 'flat port', which is, I believe, what some wine men label Tarragona. I also remember being invited about twenty years ago to taste a glass of excellent raspberry wine, of the 1951 vintage, by Mrs McWilliam of Orchard Cottage in Bakewell. She had made it herself, and was also good enough to give me her recipe for a traditional Moorland Tart.

Take 2 *eggs, boiled hard* and shelled and fairly finely chopped, both the yolk and the white part. You also need 75*g* (3 *oz*) *butter*, 100*g* (4 *oz*) *sugar*, 100*g* (4 *oz*) *chopped peel*, 100*g* (4 *oz*) *currants, a quarter of a nutmeg freshly grated*, and some *shortcrust pastry*.

Butter a tart tin and line it with the pastry. Cream the butter and sugar until pale and fluffy, then stir in the fruit, the chopped hard-boiled eggs, and the nutmeg. Fill the pastry-lined tart tin with this mixture. Bake in a moderate oven 180°C (350°F) Gas Mark 4 until set.

Treacle Tart

Treacle tart is always made with golden syrup, though black treacle seems to have been used about a hundred years ago (and is still used for a treacle tart popular in Lincolnshire). This is an especially good recipe.

Line a tart plate with 150*g* (6 *oz*) *shortcrust pastry* and make a fluted edge or, if liked, a gable. Melt 25*g* (1 *oz*) *butter* and 3 *good tablespoons of golden syrup*. Add the *grated rind and juice of* 1 *lemon*. Stir in 3 *tablespoons soft white breadcrumbs*. Cool the mixture and add a *lightly-beaten egg*. Pour it into the pastry-lined tart plate. Lay a decorative lattice of leftover pastry strips across the tart, if liked. Bake in a fairly hot oven 190°C (375°F) Gas Mark 5 for about 30 minutes.

A gable is the pattern sometimes used in Lancashire when making tarts, when they have only one kind of jam or filling in them. Make short, but parallel, cuts about 12mm (½ in) apart all round the outside edge of the pastry case. Now fold in every alternate piece. It looks something like part of a medieval fortress, and may well be as old as castle battlements. Treacle tart is delicious for a picnic and packs very well between two plates. It also freezes beautifully.

Breadcrumbs

Nowadays one can easily make soft white breadcrumbs – for treacle tarts, and stuffings and puddings – in the electric mixer. Simply put in the pieces of fresh or stale bread, preferably without the crusts, and whizz them to crumbs. I store them, in usable quantities, in polythene bags in the freezer, ready for use.

Westmorland Threedecker

Make some *shortcrust pastry*, using 300*g* (12 *oz*) *flour* and 150*g* (6 *oz*) *butter*. Divide it in three and roll out one piece using it to line a greased tart plate. Pile 200*g* (8 *oz*) *peeled, cored, thinly-sliced apples* on the pastry, sprinkle them with 100*g* (4 *oz*) *brown sugar* and the *grated rind of half a lemon*. Damp the pastry edges with cold water, and, having rolled out another pastry round, cover the apples with it and seal the edges. Put on another layer of 200*g* (8 *oz*) *sliced apples* with 100*g* (4 *oz*) *brown sugar* and some *grated lemon rind*,

Then add a final round of pastry. Seal the edges well, pinching them together with your fingers. Trim off any surplus pastry with a sharp knife. Brush the top with milk, make slits in the top to let the steam out.

Put the tart plate on a baking tray. Bake it in a really hot oven 220°C (425°F) Gas Mark 7 for 20 minutes. Then reduce the heat to moderate 180°C (350°F) Gas Mark 4 for another 40 minutes. Take it out of the oven and sprinkle the top with brown sugar. To be eaten hot.

A Westmorland Threedecker can also be made with stoned plums or blackberries instead of the apples, or with a combination of both.

Wilfra Tarts

These are the cheesecakes and small jam tarts eaten in Ripon in Wilfra or Wilfred Week, in the first week in August, when there is a procession to commemorate St Wilfred re-entering the town. People used to get up very early to bake them and then set them on trays before the houses for passers-by to help themselves.

Jam tarts, with three or four different kinds of jam laid in them in sections, and divided by strips of pastry in fancy patterns, were the pride of some housewives, the designs being largely traditional.

Yorkshire Cheesecakes or Curd Tarts

Cheesecakes are a speciality of farms all over the Ridings, and are to be seen brown and glistening in Yorkshire bakers' shops, but they are almost unknown in other parts of Britain. Recipes vary as do the methods of making the curd cheese for them. They are delicious with a glass of well-chilled *vin rosé* or dry white wine.

Line a greased tart plate with 200*g* (8 *oz*) *shortcrust pastry*. Mix 200*g* (8 *oz*) *curds* with 100*g* (4 *oz*) *sugar*, 50*g* (2 *oz*) *currants* and 2 *well-beaten eggs*. Pour it into the pastry-lined plate. Sprinkle it with *freshly-grated nutmeg*. Bake it in a moderately hot oven 190°C (375°F) Gas Mark 5 for about 20 minutes.

In Yorkshire there are several popular ways of making curds, some cooks swear by one method and some by another. The whey left over from the curds is often used for making scones.

Warm 600ml (1 *pt*) *fresh milk*, but do not bring it to the boil, stir in *a teaspoon of Epsom salts* and stir the milk slowly until it curdles. Place a kitchen colander inside a mixing bowl, line the colander with a clean tea towel or table napkin. Pour in the curdled milk to strain out the whey.

Alternatively, the milk may be warmed to blood heat – no hotter – then add a teaspoon of rennet (sold in bottles by chemists and good grocers) and stir. Let it settle for an hour or so, then strain the curd from the whey as before.

It must be left for some hours to drip through the cloth. A third way is to put 3 *beaten eggs*, 600*ml* (1 *pt*) *milk*, and *a teaspoon salt* in a saucepan and bring it to the boil, stirring until it curdles thoroughly. Now pour it into a cloth to drain.

Curd for Tarts, with Vinegar

'I am giving you a recipe of my mother's,' Mrs J. Phillips, of Bingley, Yorkshire, wrote to me about eight years ago. 'I was 84 last February and I remember quite well her making curd tarts. She used to warm 1 *litre* (1 *quart*) *of milk* in a pan to blood heat, and put about 2 *tablespoons of vinegar* in it, to break it to make the curd. When cold, she strained the curd through a sieve. She then slipped 1 *egg* into it, 50*g* (2 *oz*) *sugar*, 50*g* (2 *oz*) *sultanas*, 50*g* (2 *oz*) *currants*, and mixed it all together. She would make little tarts, or big ones. Sometimes you can buy curd now in Yorkshire at pork butchers' shops.'

Shortcrust Pastry

Plain flour should be used for shortcrust pastry, though self-raising flour would do. Plain flour must be used though for biscuit crust pastry, which contains an egg, because the raising agents in the flour, when used with an egg, make the pastry too crumbly and rough.

Sift 200*g* (8 *oz*) *plain or self-raising flour* (8 heaped tablespoons) and *a pinch of salt* into a basin together. Cut 100*g* (4 *oz*) *not-too-hard frozen butter* in 4 chunks. Rub it into the flour with the tips of your fingers, or blend it in the electric mixer until it is like fine breadcrumbs, with no loose flour round the basin. Add 2 *tablespoons cold water* all at once, and mix it – not with your fingers but with a round-bladed knife – until the whole thing clings together and leaves the sides of the bowl clean.

FOR EXTRA-SHORT CRUST PASTRY use 125*g* (5 *oz*) *butter* and only 1 *tablespoon water*.

FOR BISCUIT CRUST PASTRY mix 200*g* (8 *oz*) *plain flour* with *a pinch of salt*. Rub in 125*g* (5 *oz*) *butter*. Mix in *a rounded dessertspoon of caster sugar* with *a dessertspoon of water* and an *egg yolk*. The rest is as before.

IX
High Tea

Eccles Cakes
Goosnargh Cakes
Muffins and Much Else
Griddle Scones
Another Singin' Hinny
Yorkshire and Durham Pikelets
Yorkshire Oven-Bottom Cake
Fidget or Fitchett Pie
Grannie Biscuits
Rock Cakes at Keld
Plain Sponge Sandwich
Yorkshire Seed Cake
Simnel Cake
Fancy Breads
Yorkshire Yule Loaf
Derbyshire Oatcakes
Roll-Up Havacake
Cut-and-Come-Again Cake
Dent
Family Fruit Cake

High Tea

High tea is a knife and fork meal eaten in Scotland and the north of England in the early evening between 5.30 and 6.30. It usually comprises ham with every possible kind of bread, scone, tea cake, sweet cake, parkin and pastry. North Country women are good providers and expect you to make a hearty meal. High tea menus and prices are quoted in the brochures of many northern hotels alongside those for dinner and it is, of course, the perfect meal after a day of grouse shooting or hunting. But it has almost vanished in the south.

It was a new and fashionable meal in London in the Naughty Nineties. Society hostesses produced a large spread of cold meats, game, custards, cakes, fresh fruit and tea, or sometimes wine, was served with it. Young people were said to prefer it to dinner as it did 'not interfere with tennis, boating and other amusements'. Those rickety Victorian bamboo tables were, it seems, made specially for high tea and, according to the 1901 edition of Mrs Beeton, when 'placed at right hand of the lady of the house would enable her to dispense the tea without leaving her place at the head of the table'.

Eccles Cakes

The original recipe is a secret and there are cake makers in Eccles who still hold this secret, though this recipe is as near to it as may be. The cakes are traditional to Lancashire, as are Nelson cakes, made with currants, Goosnargh cakes from near Preston and Simnel cakes from Bury.

Roll out some *rough puff or flaky pastry*, made with butter, into rounds about 7.5cm (3 in) across. Put *a table-spoon of the filling* in the middle of each. This is just *cur-*

rants, brown sugar, a little butter and a very small amount of *golden syrup* – too much can make the cake boil and this will spoil the taste, as anyone in Eccles will tell you.

Bunch up the fruit in the pastry to make a bag, but without gathering too much pastry to the top of this bag. Now flatten the cake, turning it over so that the folds are underneath. Brush over the top very, very lightly with water – *not* egg and *not* milk – then sprinkle a little sugar on top. Cut a small hole in the middle of the top of each. Bake them on a baking sheet in a really hot oven 220°C (425°F) Gas Mark 7 for 15–20 minutes.

Goosnargh Cakes

These are really a kind of rich biscuit, they come from a place near Preston, in Lancashire. Rub 175*g* (7 *oz*) *butter* and 25*g* (1 *oz*) *lard* into 200*g* (8 *oz*) *plain flour*, add ½ *teaspoon caraway seeds*, 1 *tablespoon caster sugar* and the *beaten white of an egg*, mix well and chill. Put the rich dough on a floured board. Roll it out 6mm (¼ in) thick, cut it out with a plain (4–5cm) (1½–2in) cutter or with the top of a wine glass. Dust the biscuits thickly with caster sugar. Bake them in a slow oven 150°C–170°C (250°F–300°F) Gas Mark 1–2 for 30–40 minutes. Dust them again with caster sugar while still hot.

Muffins and Much Else

Crumpets, muffins and pikelets of all different shapes and sizes are still sold by bakers and in street markets in the north of England. Muffins and crumpets are mostly bought ready-made, but pikelets and so on are often made at home. Muffins are now less popular than crumpets but most bakers would almost certainly make them on request. They would be very good for breakfast, hot and buttered, as well as for tea. To toast them properly pull the muffins apart with the fingers about 12mm (½ in) all round. Toast them slowly on both sides so the middle gets warm through. Stuff plenty of butter in the middle and fit them together. Serve them in a muffineer with hot water in the space below, or wrapped in a muffin cloth. The old British muffin, now going out of fashion in England, is much enjoyed on the other side of the Atlantic. Some are made there, some are air lifted from Britain. The Americans are very fond of them hot at dinner and breakfast.

We also export quantities of frozen crumpets to the United States. The familiar English crumpet is delicious when toasted on both sides, the smooth side first and the side with the holes last, then buttered thickly over the holes until they are like little wells of butter, soggy, fattening and luscious.

Griddle Scones

In Northumberland these are eaten hot with butter. They are sometimes called Singin' Hinnies. Mix 200*g* (8 *oz*) *flour* with ½ *teaspoon salt*. Rub in 50*g* (2 *oz*) lard and 50*g* (2 *oz*) *butter*, adding 1 *teaspoon baking powder* and 25g (1 *oz*) *currants*. Mix it to a soft dough with *a little cream or thick sour milk* – it must not be too soft. Roll it out 6mm (¼ in) thick and cut it into rounds with the top of a tumbler. Have ready a hot very lightly-greased griddle or frying-pan. Bake them on it on both sides. When nicely coloured on one side turn them to cook the other. These are delicious hot and split with butter.

Another Singin' Hinny

These are also known as Farmhouse Griddle Cakes. Mix 300*g* (12 *oz*) *flour*, 50*g* (2 *oz*) *ground rice*, 1 *teaspoon salt* and 50*g* (2 *oz*) *sugar*. Add 2 *teaspoons baking powder* and rub in 25*g* (1 *oz*) *lard*. Mix in 75*g* (3 *oz*) *currants*. Then add 150*ml* (¼ *pt*) *half thick cream and half milk*, mixing it all to a moderately soft dough. Roll it out 6mm (¼ in) thick. Prick it all over with a fork and bake it on a fairly hot and lightly-greased griddle, turning until nicely browned on both sides.

It can be cut in halves or quarters for convenience in turning.

Yorkshire and Durham Pikelets

These are very good for tea. They are served hot and buttered piled up on a plate under a warm folded napkin or muffin cloth.

Sift 200*g* (8 *oz*) *flour* with 50*g* (2 *oz*) *caster sugar* and *a good pinch of salt* into a basin. Get some *buttermilk* from the milkman, and little by little stir in about 125ml (¼ pt) of it, just enough to make a thick batter.

Melt 1 *teaspoon bicarbonate of soda* in 2 *tablespoons of boiling water*, stir this in too. Now grease a frying-pan and get it hot. Take a tablespoon and drop the batter on to the hot pan in rounds from the spoon, but keep them a bit apart as they spread.

Fry your pikelets until they are brown below and bubbly on top, then turn them with a fish slice and fry the other side. Put plenty of butter on them and eat them before they are cold.

Yorkshire Oven-Bottom Cake

Yorkshire oven-bottom cake used to be made at the end of baking day, having been put into the bottom of the oven when the loaves were taken out. When cooked, it was taken from the oven, wrapped in a tea towel and placed on a cushion. To serve, it was cut or broken in irregular pieces, split, and spread thick with butter or jam.

Put a 100*g* (4 *oz*) *lump of bread dough* on a pastry board. Cut 25*g* (1 *oz*) *lard* into 6 pieces, press roughly into the dough and fold this over. Press the lard into the dough with the knuckles of one hand, making it look all lumpy. Bake it on a greased baking sheet in a very hot oven 230°C (450°F) Gas Mark 8 for about 15 minutes until golden.

Fidget or Fitchett Pie

This is eaten hot with sugar, for High Tea in Cheshire and Shropshire, usually with cheese as well. Cheese is almost always eaten with any apple pie in the north of England – a piece of blue or red Cheshire would be delicious with fitchett. Of course Yorkshire people generally say White Wensleydale, a soft acid cheese, is the very one for apple pie. Tastes differ.

'But I, when I undress me
Each night upon my knees
Will ask the Lord to bless me,
With apple pie and cheese.'

Fitchett pie must go back hundreds of years. Mrs Glasse, writing in 1749, gives a very similar version of it she called Cheshire Pork Pie. Hers is made with apples, pork and white wine, but is obviously closely related.

Skin, peel and core 4 *apples*, put them in a pie dish. Cover the apples with *peeled sliced onions*, then a layer of *chopped bacon*. Continue thus, in layers till the dish is full. Add a *heaped teaspoon (or tablespoon) of sugar*, depending on the tartness of the apples. Add also a good tablespoon of water and a pie funnel. Cover the pie dish with *rough puff or shortcrust pastry*. Brush this with milk or a beaten egg.

Bake it in a hot oven 200°C (400°F) Gas Mark 6 for rough puff, a moderate oven 180°C (350°F) Gas Mark 4 for shortcrust, until the pastry is brown and looks cooked and the apples are soft when speared with a skewer. Pots of strong tea, thick slices of fresh home-baked bread and farm butter go with it beautifully.

Grannie Biscuits

Home-made biscuits have more snob value and usually taste better as well as being cheaper than the factory kind. Most are easy to make, and the biscuit dough also freezes very well. In Lancashire this kind of biscuit is sometimes called a Shrewsbury biscuit, and I have also seen them, hand-made and prettily hand-packed, labelled 'Bronte Biscuits, as made at Haworth parsonage'.

Sift 200g (8 *oz*) *plain flour* with 1 *teaspoon baking powder.* Rub in 100g (4 *oz*) *butter* until the mixture is like fine crumbs. This may be done in the electric mixer, if liked. Stir in 150g (6 *oz*) *caster sugar*, then, either 50g (2 *oz*) *finely-chopped shelled walnuts or a few currants.* Add *a beaten egg* and mix it all to a smooth pastry-like dough. The best cooks now turn it out on to a floured pastry board and knead the dough for about 2 minutes, before wrapping it in foil and chilling it for 15 minutes in the refrigerator.

The dough may, if liked, be rolled out and cut in rounds with the top of a wine glass. Some cooks keep back about 25g (1 oz) of the sugar to sprinkle on the top when rolling it out. Or you can shape it into a long 'sausage', 5cm (2 in) thick. Cut it in slices 12mm (½ in) thick and put these on a buttered or oiled baking sheet.

Bake them in a fairly hot oven 190°C (375°F) Gas Mark 5 for 10 minutes, or until the Grannie biscuits are turning a nice golden colour. Leave them for 2 minutes. Then take them out and cool them on a wire rack. They should be stored in a tin.

TO FREEZE THE BISCUIT DOUGH Wrap the 5cm (2 in) thick 'sausage' in foil and freeze it. Later unwrap the dough, before baking, and thaw it for one hour in the refrigerator, then slice and bake it as before.

Rock Cakes at Keld

Talking of Wensleydale cheeses takes me back to the early thirties when, unemployed and with only a few bob in my pocket, I tramped the Yorkshire dales. For sheer generosity no one I met in those lonely parts equalled, or even came near to the great-hearted little woman who ran the 'Cat-hole Inn' at Keld in Wensleydale. Mrs Hutchinson had also known hard times. She also had a keen eye and, within minutes of my arrival, dusty and foot-blistered, I was sat down before a vast plate of home-cured ham, soft crumbling cheese, home-baked bread and the local brewer's dark brown ale. Believe it or not, Mrs Hutchinson saw to it that I sat down every evening to this self-same feast – and it was a feast – as anticipated on the last day as unanticipated on the first. On Sunday the feast finished with a treat – tinned peaches and cream from the 'Cat-hole' cow. And I am forgetting! There was also tomato sandwiches, home-made rock cakes with raspberry jam (yes, home-made) and steaming boats of brown tea. You know, there was small variety in the food available in that remote dale, but what there was I have never since tasted the equal of. God bless you Mrs Hutchinson up there among the angels with your treasured pile of willow-pattern plates.

I had this charming letter from Mr Siegel of North London. He seemed surprised when I told him he had been given 'high tea' but did remember the rock cakes as 'different'. The recipe, I imagine, must be this unusual one.

Rub 150*g* (6 *oz*) *unsalted butter* into 350*g* (14 *oz*) *plain flour*, then add 50*g* (2 *oz*) *lightly-toasted fine breadcrumbs*, 75*g* (3 *oz*) *brown sugar*, 2 *teaspoons baking powder* and 1 *egg beaten with a little milk*. Sometimes 150*g* (6 *oz*) *moist currants* are added.

Mix all together to a stiff dough, spoon out rough 'rocks' on to a floured baking sheet and cook for 15–20 minutes at 200°C (400°F) Gas Mark 6.

Keld, by the way, is a tiny hamlet, said to have been founded by the Vikings.

Plain Sponge Sandwich

It is a very strange thing, but some otherwise very good cooks are hopeless at making a sponge sandwich. Here is a very easy recipe for this popular cake. It would be delicious sandwiched with marrow and pineapple jam, or lemon curd or rum butter. It freezes well.

You need two 18cm (7 in) sandwich tins. Butter and line the bottom with buttered foil or greaseproof paper. Put 100*g* (4 *oz*) *softened butter* in a mixing bowl with 100*g* (4 *oz*) *caster sugar*, 2 *eggs*, the *grated rind of a lemon*, 100*g* (4 *oz*) *selfraising flour* which you have sifted together with 1 *level teaspoon baking powder*. Beat all these in the electric mixer or with a wooden spoon till smooth in about two minutes. Pour it into your sandwich tins. Bake the two halves of the cake on the middle shelf of a fairly cool oven 170°C (325°F) Gas Mark 3 for 25–30 minutes. Cool them on a wire rack.

Yorkshire Seed Cake

Line and grease 20cm (8 in) round cake tin. Cream 150*g* (6*oz*) *softened butter* with 150*g* (6*oz*) *caster sugar* thoroughly for 3 or 4 minutes until light and fluffy. Add the *grated rind of half a lemon* and 25*g* (1 *oz*) *caraway seeds*. Beat in 3 *whole eggs* one at a time, adding *a tablespoon plain flour*. Gently fold in the rest of the flour 200g (8 oz) altogether, sieved together with *a teaspoon baking powder*. Fold it in with a large metal spoon. Transfer it to the prepared tin and smooth the top with a knife. Sprinkle it with sugar and a few caraway seeds before putting it in the centre of a very moderate oven 170°C (325°F) Gas Mark 3 for 1½–1¾ hours. Leave it in the tin for 5 minutes then turn it out on to a wire cooling rack. Carefully peel off the paper when the cake is cold. Store the cake in an airtight tin.

Simnel Cake

Simnel Cake is associated with Simnel or Mid-Lent Sunday in the north and with Easter Sunday in the south. Mothering, or Mid-Lent Sunday was a religious festival in the Middle Ages in honour of Mary, Mother of Jesus. By the eighteenth century it had become the time, at Mid-Lent, when servants and apprentices hired out to farmers at the previous Mop Fair, or others who had long been in service, visited their parents taking gifts of food. The gift was often a cake given by their employer, a Simnel Cake, which comes originally from Bury in Lancashire. The practice of making them in the middle of Lent goes back in tradition about four hundred years. Mid-Lent Sunday was sometimes called 'Braggot' Sunday because mulled or spiced ale called Braggot was drunk on that day.

Brush a 23cm (9 in) cake tin with cooking oil and line it with oiled paper. Cream 200g (8 *oz*) *butter* and 200g (8 *oz*) *brown sugar* together, adding the *grated rind of a lemon.* Sift 200g (8 *oz*) *flour* with *a pinch of salt, ¾ teaspoon baking powder, a teaspoon mixed spice.* Sprinkle a little of the flour mixture over the creamed butter and sugar, add *four eggs* – one at a time with a teaspoon of flour between each. Beat well between each egg. Fold the rest of the flour into the egg mixture. Add the fruit last – 400g (1 *lb*) *sultanas,* 200g (8 *oz*) *currants,* 100g (4 *oz*) *chopped peel,* 50g (2 *oz*) *chopped almonds,* 100g (4 *oz*) *halved glacé cherries.* Add just enough *milk* to give a stiff batter.

Turn half the mixture into the oiled and papered tin, smooth the top with a knife and having rolled about a third of your *marzipan* into a round to fit the tin, lay it on top. Cover it with the rest of your cake mixture and press it down lightly with a wooden spoon. Bake it in a slow oven 150°C (300°F) Gas Mark 2 for about 3½ hours. It is done when a skewer thrust into the cake comes out clean and dry. Only don't stick it into the marzipan or you may be misled. When done, let it cool slightly. Brush round the top with *apricot jam or redcurrant jelly.* Lay a second circle of marzipan on top pressing it down well. Notch the edge with fingers and thumb like a pie crust, and mark it in squares with a knife. With the trimmings make 11 marzipan balls, arrange them round the edge like a peer's coronet. Brush over lightly with beaten egg. Bake in a fairly slow oven 170°C (325°F) Gas Mark 3 for 20 minutes to toast the marzipan.

Let it stand for 20 minutes then turn it out gently, base down, marzipan on top, on a wire rack. Run a little green or yellow water ice in the centre to form a sort of lake.

TO MAKE YOUR OWN MARZIPAN Mix 200*g* (8 *oz*) *ground almonds*, 200*g* (8 *oz*) *sifted icing sugar*, the *juice of half a lemon* and *one or two beaten eggs*, enough to make a firm paste. Knead this well with the fingers until smooth, and roll it out as required.

Fancy Breads

Many of the fruit loaves of the north are intended to be eaten with cheese and are especially associated with Christmas, though some were intended for Sunday-school treats. They are often sliced and buttered. Spiced bread has been served at Christmas together with the Christmas Ale for many years in the Tap Room of one old Yorkshire coaching inn near Moos and Fenwich and has now become a tradition of the house.

These breads would be delicious too for a continental breakfast, the kind one has in Norway, Denmark and Holland with four or five different fancy breads, some hot from the oven, and with cheese to go with them.

Yorkshire Yule Loaf

Put 600*g* (1½ *lb*) *plain flour*, 2 *teaspoons baking powder* and a small *teaspoon salt* in a mixing bowl and rub in 100*g* (4 *oz*) *butter* and 100*g* (4 *oz*) *lard* until the mixture is like fine crumbs. Now add 400*g* (1 *lb*) *sugar*, 400*g* (1 *lb*) *small stoned raisins*, 200*g* (8 *oz*) *currants*, 50*g* (2 *oz*), *candied peel* and *freshly-grated nutmeg* to your taste. Cream 50*g* (2 *oz*) *fresh yeast* in a small basin with *a little sugar*. Add 250*ml* (½ *pt*) *warm milk* and *a well-beaten egg*. Mix all this into the dough. Put it to rise in two greased loaf tins for an hour, covered with a cloth and leave in a pleasantly warm room until well risen. Bake them in a moderate oven 180°C (350°F) Gas Mark 4 for 45 minutes.

Derbyshire Oatcakes

These are a sort of large luscious muffin or pancake, popular all over Derbyshire and parts of Staffordshire as well as in Yorkshire. I was given this recipe about twenty-five years ago by Mrs Bloomer at the baker's and confectioner's shop in Bakewell.

You eat them fried in bacon dip for breakfast, or toasted and buttered thickly, or with a fried egg on top, or with some black pudding or sausages. They are closer to a Breton pancake than to the oatcakes made in Scotland. They can be bought from the local baker.

Mix 200*g* (8 *oz*) *wholemeal flour*, 400*g* (1 *lb*) *Scotch oatmeal* and 15*g* (½ *oz*) *baking powder*. Warm about 1 litre (2 pt) *water* to 28°C (90°F) – just under blood heat. Add to it 15*g* (½ *oz*) *salt* and 25*g* (1 *oz*) *crumbled fresh yeast*. Stir it well. Then add the dry ingredients gradually, stirring and beating the mixture well until you have something like a Yorkshire pudding batter.

Let it stand in a warm place for 20 minutes to 'work'. If it drops down, stir it up again. If the mixture seems too thin, add a very little more oatmeal, if it seems too thick, add a little warm water or warm milk. Lightly grease a hot-plate, or an oven shelf, or a proper metal griddle, and when it is hot pour a small teacupful of the mixture on to the centre. Cook it for about 5 minutes, then turn the oatcake over and cook the other side. Turn it back to the first side for 2 minutes and then put it on a wire sieve to cool.

These cakes keep for two or three days until you are ready to fry them.

Roll-Up Havacake

'Another associate of cheese is the thin flat oatcake, sold in large oval sheets about twice the size of a pancake, and just as soft,' wrote Donald Boyd in *On Foot In Yorkshire* 1932. 'My grandmother used to hang them over a string in front of the fire to dry, but I preferred them soft, covered with butter and treacle, and rolled up like a truncheon. A famous regiment is called after those oatcakes, the Roll-up Havercake Lads.'

Cut-and-Come-Again Cake

Anyone who has visited Dentdale, which is really the lovely valley of the River Dee, will remember J. Dinsdale and Sons, grocers, drapers, irongmongers, corn and provision merchants at The Stores in Main Street, tucked in among the narrow cobbled streets and grey stone cottages of Dent. Sadly J. Dinsdale and Sons are no longer bakers, having closed down the bakehouse some five years ago. But Mr J. R. Goodyear, one of the four directors, was good enough to send me this recipe for their famous cake.

Grease a large cake tin and line it with paper. See that the oven is moderately hot 180°C (350°F) Gas Mark 4. Put 1 *tablespoon golden syrup*, 200g (8 *oz*) *margarine* and 375 *ml* (¾ *pt*) *milk* into a saucepan and sit it by the side of the fire. Stir occasionally until the mixture is smooth and well blended. Put all the dry ingredients in a large mixing bowl – 100g (4 *oz*) *sultanas*, 200g (8 *oz*) *currants*, 50g (2 *oz*) *candied peel*, chopped, 50g (2 *oz*) *Demerara sugar*, 400g (1 *lb*) *self-raising flour* and 150g (6 *oz*) *granulated sugar*. Mix them thoroughly. Then add the contents of the saucepan and beat well. Pour it into the prepared tin and bake the cake in a moderate oven 180°C (350°F) Gas Mark 4 for 2–3 hours. Do not open the door for 30 minutes after putting the cake in. Try it with a clean warm steel knitting-needle. If this comes out clean the cake is done. When finished remove from the oven and let it stay in the tin for another 30 minutes. Do not put it into a cold larder whilst it is still hot.

Dent

While on the subject of Dent I had this letter from a reader and print it without comment:

'Just after the First World War my father acquired a "bull-nosed" Morris motor car. Every Sunday in summer the family went for a "spin". I well remember the first time we drove through Dent, in Dentdale, Yorkshire. My young brother yelled, "Look! Men knitting!" What scorn he put into "knitting"!

'Indeed, men were sitting outside their cottage doors knitting – gloves, scarves, tammies in black and red wool, with, as I remember, zig-zag patterns. Sadly, on subsequent visits the number of cottagers knitting outside declined, and then there were none. I suppose the rude shouts of small boys and the dust and smell of noisy motor cars drove the cottagers within doors.

'Years later, finding myself once again in Dent I inquired of a very old lady about those "men knitting". Shyly, and after some prompting, she opened a drawer and showed me a pair of exquisite knitted gloves in black and red wool. "Those are the last pair my husband knitted before he died," she said sadly.' From Mrs Turner, of Leeds.

Family Fruit Cake

This is very popular in Leeds and the West Riding for high tea. It is sometimes called luncheon cake and also cut-and-come-again cake, like the previous one. In Yorkshire you often get a slice of Wensleydale cheese and a slice of cake on your plate at the same time.

A little bit of spice and a little bit of cheese,
A glass of cold water and a penny if you please'

go the words of the old Yorkshire rhyme.

Mrs Bolton, head of the Homecraft Department of the Thomas Danby Technical College in Leeds, whose recipe you see on p. 126, once told me that the rhyme is really part of an old temperance song. There was something in the first verse, Mrs Bolton says, about not drinking beer.

This kind of old-fashioned slab or luncheon cake was once made for sportsmen and farm workers to take in the pocket with their lunch sandwiches when out walking, shooting or working far from home. Nowadays many people run a car and can come home for lunch, but walking used to take too long, especially if you were working in a remote part of the farm. They took their dinner in 'bait' baskets.

Rub 150*g* (6 *oz*) *soft butter* into 250*g* (10 *oz*) *selfraising flour*. Then add 150*g* (6 *oz*) *soft brown sugar*, 150*g* (6 *oz*) *sultanas*, 100*g* (4 *oz*) *currants*, 75*g* (3 *oz*) *stoned raisins*, 25*g* (1 *oz*) *chopped candied peel* and ¼ *teaspoon of powdered cinnamon*. Then just mix it all to a soft consistency with 4 *beaten eggs* and *a little milk*. Some cooks add a tablespoon of rum or brandy to the mixture and some do not. Mrs Bolton says, 'It is one of those free-and-easy recipes where you can vary the ingredients a bit as you like it.' Put it in a prepared 20cm (8 in) cake tin. Bake it in a moderate oven 180°C (350°F) Gas Mark 4 for 1½ hours.

X
Jams, Sauces, Pickles and Vinegar

Bilberry and Rhubarb Jam
Elderflower and Gooseberry Jelly
Bramble and Sloe Jelly
Marrow and Ginger Jam
Simple Marrow and Ginger Jam
Marrow and Pineapple Jam
Orange Pickle
Rhubarb, Ginger and Chopped Peel Jam
Rum Butter
Another Cumberland Recipe
Sugar Thermometers
Cumberland Sauce
North Country Gooseberry Sauce
Raspberry Vinegar

Jams, Sauces, Pickles and Vinegar

One of the pleasures of making jam is being able to use the huge brass jam pan I once bought from an antique shop in Richmond, Yorkshire. It is very heavy, has a rigid handle over the top and the outside is all blackened by what must be centuries of wood smoke. Hung up in the kitchen it is most impressive, but in action on the cooker (even though the bottom is curved and obviously intended for hanging over open fires) it looks amazing.

Most old brass jam pans make lovely jam – if they are stained inside clean them with a scouring powder and hot water, but do not *ever* use them for pickles or anything with vinegar in it as this attacks the brass with nasty results. Jam, by the way, will hardly need skimming and will not froth up and boil over if you add about a teaspoon of butter to the pan of fruit and sugar. Of course home-made jam is worth making partly because it tastes better, and, if you grow your own fruit, it is also cheaper. You can also make gorgeous jams that you never see in shops . . . oh, the vulgar snobbery of it!

Bilberry and Rhubarb Jam

Take 1.25*kg* (3 *lb*) *bilberries*, 1.25*kg* (3 *lb*) *sugar*, 1 *tablespoon water*. Pick over the bilberries, put fruit, sugar and water in a basin and leave them for 24 hours, till the juice runs. Add 200*g* (8 *oz*) *chopped rhubarb* (or the juice of a lemon) to help the jam to set. Tip it all into a jam pan. Boil until setting point is reached. Bottle in warm jars, cover them when cold.

SETTING POINT To see if the jam or jelly is set, pour about ¼ teaspoon on to a cold saucer. As it cools, it should thicken and wrinkle if you push it with a spoon.

Elderflower and Gooseberry Jelly

This subtle conserve has a flavour like muscat grapes or warm geraniums. Cover the *gooseberries* with *water* and let them simmer for 2 hours; they need not be topped and tailed. Strain off the juice without squeezing the pulpy fruit as this will make the jelly cloudy. Add 400*g* (1 *lb*) *sugar* to each 600*ml* (1 *pt*) *juice*. Stir, heating gently until the sugar melts. Add 12 *big heads of elderflowers* tied together in a bunch in a muslin bag. Elderflower is that common English tree growing everywhere in the hedgerows and in flower when gooseberries are in season. Bring it all to the boil in your jam pan, boil for 10 minutes, test for setting (see page 129). Bottle it in warm jars and cover them when cold.

Some people cut up a lemon and cook it with the gooseberries, instead of elderflowers, others add geranium leaves (pelargonium) to the pan of fruit. Both flavours are good.

Bramble and Sloe Jelly

Add 100*g* (4 *oz*) *sloes* to every 400*g* (1 *lb*) *blackberries*, pricking the sloes before cooking them. Continue as for other jellies.

Marrow and Ginger Jam

'I have been a housekeeper a good few years,' writes Miss Eva Buckley of Southport in Lancashire, 'and this is how I used to make the marrow jam for a lady up to the last war when I was under the doctor. Of course things were a good bit cheaper in those days.

'Peel the *marrow* and chop it in pieces without the seeds and pith. Weigh it and add 1.5*kg* (4 *lb*) *sugar* to every 1.5*kg* (4 *lb*) *marrow pieces*. Leave it in a basin covered with a cloth for 24 hours together with the *juice of* 2 *lemons and the rind*, cut fine without any of the white part. Add as well 40*g* (1½ *oz*) *best root ginger* and ½ *teaspoon Cayenne pepper* (or to taste) tied in a muslin. Bring it to the boil in your jam pan, bubbling very gently for $1\frac{1}{2}$ hours. Stir occasionally. When it is transparent add 2 *wineglasses of whisky.*'

Simple Marrow and Ginger Jam

'This makes very good jam and is handy as it is made with ground ginger which you can usually get from the corner shop even if you cannot buy the root or crystallized ginger usually specified.' So writes Mrs E. G. Taylor, of Wigan, in Lancashire.

'Peel the *marrow* and cut it in squares. Put 2.5*kg* (6*lb*) *sugar* to 2.75*kg* (7 *lb*) *marrow* in a big basin with 50*g* (2 *oz*) *ground ginger* (or to taste) and the *rind and juice of* 4 *lemons.* Let it stand for 3 whole days giving it a stir each day, then tip it in the jam pan, bring it to the boil, then let it boil just in its own juice until the marrow is quite soft, the syrup has thickened and setting point is reached. It should be done gently and may take about 2 hours.'

Marrow and Pineapple Jam

This is very delicious, goes well with an old-fashioned rice pudding, and makes a good filling for a sandwich cake.

Peel *a large marrow* and cut it into chunks without the seeds and centre part. Large overgrown courgettes may be used if more convenient. Put 1.25*kg* (3 *lb*) *sugar* to every 1.5*kg* (4 *lb*) prepared marrow and leave it until next day for the juices to run out of it, adding the contents of *a large tin of pineapple chunks.* Put it in a jam pan and bring it gently to the boil, stirring until all the sugar has melted. If necessary, break down the chunks with a wooden spoon. Then boil, not too rapidly, until the setting point is reached.

Bottle it in warm jars and cover when cold.

Orange Pickle

This is a delicate spicy pickle which used to be made in Cheshire. It is very good with cheese or with cold roast duck.

Peel 6 *oranges* and slice them thickly, taking out the pips and cutting away the pith. Steam them in the top of a double pan till they are clear, soft and translucent. In another saucepan simmer *two cups of distilled white vinegar* with some pieces of *stick cinnamon, cloves* and *mace*, and also *a strip of lemon peel*, tied in a bit of muslin. Add 3 *cups of white sugar*, bring it to the boil gradually, stirring until the sugar has melted. Boil for 25 minutes before removing the spice bag. Add the fruit, simmer for at least an hour. Bottle as usual and leave it at least 3 weeks before using.

Rhubarb, Ginger and Chopped Peel Jam

Rhubarb used to be called the Spring Fruit, and 'rhubarb for Easter' is an old country slogan. Though by April people are often eating the outdoor rhubarb, those thin pink delicately-flavoured rhubarb stalks on sale in January are from forced rhubarb – very probably from near Leeds where it is grown commercially. Champagne Early is a famous variety of bright scarlet early rhubarb.

For the jam, trim, de-string and chop 2.5*kg* (6 *lb*) *garden rhubarb* – late season's coarse rhubarb will do. Put it in a basin with 2.5*kg* (6 *lb*) *sugar*, cover this with a tea towel and leave it for 24 hours. It will then be swimming in fragrant pink juice. Strain this into a pan. Boil it for 10 minutes and pour it back over the rhubarb. Add 150*g* (6 *oz*) *mixed, chopped peel* and *a piece of root ginger*, bruised. Leave it for another 24 hours. Now bring it to the boil in your jam pan and boil it rapidly until setting point is reached. Remove the ginger before potting the jam.

Rum Butter

Everyone knows that rum butter is delicious with Christmas pudding, but it is also very good for tea on brown bread and butter.

In Cumberland it used to be eaten often on cream crackers, oatcakes or plain biscuits to celebrate the birth of a baby. Cumberland housewives make large quantities of rum butter, ready for visitors. It also makes a good filling for pancakes or a sponge sandwich cake.

Melt 400g (1 *lb*) *butter*, add 600g (1½ *lb*) *soft brown 'pieces' sugar*, add 2 *teaspoons of freshly-grated nutmeg* and pour in a good *wineglass of rum*. Mix well until it begins to set, pour it into a pretty china bowl and leave it to set.

ANOTHER CUMBERLAND RECIPE Beat 200g (8 *oz*) *unsalted butter* to a cream. Add 400g (1 *lb*) *caster sugar* and *a little grated nutmeg*. Beat it well until quite smooth and it is dropping off the spoon, add *a wineglass of rum*. Mix well. Put it in your best bowl and use it when set.

Sugar Thermometers

If making a lot of toffee or jam it is worth buying a sugar thermometer. These usually have a clip to fasten them to the side of the jam pan or toffee pan. They usually show from 100°C–316°C (212°F–500°F) though not all sugar thermometers register as high as 316°C (500°F). Fat thermometers do though and can be used for sugar work too.

SUGAR TEMPERATURES

114°C – 238°F – Soft ball
123°C – 254°F – Hard ball
143°C – 290°F – Crack or bubble
177°C – 350°F – Caramel

Cumberland Sauce

An historic sauce from a farmhouse recipe for serving with cold ham, cold venison or any other cold game and with roast goose and duck.

Add the strained *juice of an orange and a lemon and the grated rind of both* to 200g (8 *oz*) *redcurrant jelly*. Heat, stirring until it almost boils, adding *a small stick fresh-grated horseradish*. Mix well and add *half a tumbler port*.

Some people add a few glacé cherries. The sauce is bottled and served cold; it keeps for weeks in a cool dry place. If the fresh horseradish is unavailable, do not, please, use the dried kind, add a dash of Cayenne pepper and of Worcestershire sauce instead. Taste it to see if the seasoning is to your liking.

North Country Gooseberry Sauce

'The old North Country Gooseberry Sauce is delicious with bacon, ham or cold meats,' Mrs Johnson of Hexham in Northumberland once told me. 'Put 800*g* (2 *lb*) *Demerara sugar* and 500*ml* (1 *pt*) *vinegar* in an enamel pan with 1.25*kg* (3 *lb*) *topped and tailed gooseberries*, add 6*g* (¼ *oz*) *ground cloves*. Bring it all gently to the boil, stirring, until the sugar melts, then boil until it thickens in about 40 minutes. Bottle and seal.'

Raspberry Vinegar

This is used as a sauce with batter pudding, while amazingly it also makes a very good sweet-sour sauce for ice cream.

Add 500*ml* (1 *pt*) *malt vinegar* to every pound *fresh ripe raspberries*. Put it in a china bowl covered with a clean tea towel and leave it for between three days and five days. Then strain off the liquid through a double muslin, laid, if convenient, in a colander placed over a large basin. Add 400*g* (1 *lb*) *caster sugar* for every pint of liquid. Boil this for 10 minutes – but *not* in a brass jam pan because it will be attacked by the vinegar. Use an enamelled or stainless steel pan. Pour the raspberry vinegar into sterilized bottles.

Blackberry vinegar is good too. French Raspberry Vinegar is also sold in bottles by Messrs Jacksons of Piccadilly, London, W1. It is bottled by Fauchon de Paris.

XI
Sweets and Toffee

Mint Humbugs
Bulls' Eyes
Buttered Sops
Cinder Toffee
Doncaster Butterscotch
Aunt Maggie's Cough Candy
Everton Toffee
Pink Sugar Mice
Milk Toffee
Kendal Mint Cake
Russian Toffee
Toffee Apples
Treacle Toffee
Plot Toffee

Sweets and Toffee

The smell of liquorice used to greet you, dark and strong, in the village shop of my childhood. I never cared for it. I would creep in for my copy of 'Chicks' Own' and the whole place would be full of what I can only describe as black liquorice bootlaces. I don't know what they were really, I have never eaten one, however, as I raised my head to see over the counter there'd be an unmistakable odour, not of sanctity, but of lovely peppermint from the humbugs at the back of the shop. Remember mint humbugs? Those broad black and white striped things, absolutely delicious, and so huge they made your eyes water and filled your mouth so you could not speak. Mint humbugs and home-made treacle toffee are the very substance of a North Country childhood.

Mint Humbugs

Put 400*g* (1 *lb*) *Demerara sugar,* 250*ml* (½ *pt*) *water,* 50*g* (2 *oz*) *butter, a pinch of cream of tartar* and 4 *drops of oil of peppermint* in a pan. Boil it (to 143°C or 290°F on the sugar thermometer) until it forms a fine thread which can easily be snapped when you drop a little in cold water.

Take it off the heat and leave it in a pan to cool for a few minutes, then pour it on an oiled slab.

When it is cool enough to handle, pull it in long strips. For plain humbugs simply cut these in small pieces, then store them in an airtight tin.

If they are wanted striped, use the same recipe but when the toffee is on the oiled slab divide it in half, pulling one half of the mixture until it becomes much paler than the other half. Put the two strips together and roll or twist them together to make a striped effect. Cut this in short humbug lengths as before. Store the humbugs in a tin.

Bulls' Eyes

These are even larger than Mint Humbugs, and round of course. Put 1.5*kg* (3½*lb*) *soft sugar* and 500*ml* (1 *pt*) *water* in a large pan. Cook it over a low heat to melt the sugar, then boil it to 310°F–315°F.

Take the pan off the heat, stir in 7 *drops of oil of peppermint.* Pour the mixture on to an oiled slab. Cut a piece off the mass of toffee. Put it over a toffee hook and pull it until it is light brown, then pull it into lengths about 12mm (½ in) thick, keeping the mixture warm all the time. Roll it into balls and when cold put them in airtight bottles.

Buttered Sops

These are firm favourites in the Lake District. This is an extract from *Recipes of Lakeland* (Dalesman Publishing Co. of Clapham via Lancaster).

Place some half slices of *white bread* edgewise in a flat-bottomed pan (a jam pan is best). Melt 6 *oz butter*, or according to the bread prepared. Pour it over 12 *oz fine sugar* previously diluted with a small quantity of *rum* and mix well. Hang the pan containing the bread over a slow fire and pour the mixture of butter and sugar over it. Let it simmer slowly until the bread is covered, taking care not to allow it to burn, also to have the mixture equally distributed. When the bread is sufficiently moistened and the mixture is absorbed, place it on a flat dish and leave it till cold. The bread must be about half an inch thick.

Cinder Toffee

Some people call this Honeycomb Toffee but it is known as Cinder Toffee in Newcastle and the North. Put 300*g* (12 *oz*) *caster sugar*, 200*g* (8 *oz*) *golden syrup*, 50*g* (2 *oz*) *butter* and 1 *teaspoon vinegar* in a large thick pan. Heat it all gently till the sugar melts then boil it briskly for four or five minutes until it reaches 143°C (290°F on the sugar thermometer), and is at the crack or brittle stage.

Take it off the heat and add enough *bicarbonate of soda* to make it froth up and rise in the pan in a honeycomb texture. Do not boil it after adding the bicarbonate of soda. Pour it into a buttered 18cm (7 in) square tin to set. When it has cooled mark it in squares and break it into squares when cold.

Doncaster Butterscotch

Melt 400*g* (1 *lb*) *Demerara sugar* in 125*ml* (¼ *pt*) *water* in a large thick pan, then bring it to the boil and boil without stirring until it reaches 280°F on the sugar thermometer, so it forms a fine thread that can be snapped easily if you drop a little in cold water.

Stir in 50*g* (2 *oz*) *butter*, little by little. Pour it into a buttered 18cm (7 in) square tin. Mark it in squares when cool. Store in a tin. It should be wrapped in waxed paper.

Aunt Maggie's Cough Candy

An old Lancashire favourite, some people swear by this one. I loathe it, first because of the taste of the liquorice and second because of the aniseed, which I do not like either.

Put 400*g* (1 *lb*) *sugar*, ½ *cup water* and 1 *cup black treacle* in a thick heavy pan. Heat it gently stirring until the sugar melts, then boil it gently for about 10 minutes, stirring occasionally. Drop a little into cold water. If it hardens, the toffee is ready. Add 2 *drops liquorice* and 2–3 *drops oil of aniseed*. Stir well, then pour it into a buttered tin. When it is cool enough to handle, pull the toffee until it is light in colour. Then roll it into a stick and cut it into pieces with scissors.

Everton Toffee

Popular for church bazaars. The amount given in the recipe makes five quarter-pound bags of toffee.

Put 125*ml* (¼ *pt*) *water*, 1 *tablespoon golden syrup*, 400*g*

(1 *lb*) *sugar* and ¼ *teaspoon cream of tartar or vinegar* in a good thick pan. Heat it gently stirring until the sugar melts. Then bring it to the boil and boil it gently until it goes a bit darker. Now add 50–100*g* (2–4 *oz*) *butter* and boil it to a crisp. Pour it into a buttered tin and mark it into squares before it is cold.

Pink Sugar Mice

Sift 300*g* (12*oz*) *icing sugar* into a basin. Add *the white of an egg* and 50*g* (2 *oz*) *golden syrup* and mix it all with a wooden spoon. Add *one or two drops cochineal*, or confectioners' red colouring, for pink mice, mixing in the first drop of colour before adding the next so the mixture is not too dark. For white sugar mice leave the mixture plain. Then gradually add more icing sugar until the mixture is like pastry dough. Shape it into mice. Add paper, or sugar, ears, a string tail and two silver balls for eyes. Leave the mice to dry on a paper sprinkled with cornflour.

This is a recipe suitable for quite small children, since there is no fear of burning oneself.

Milk Toffee

Put 600*g* (1½ *lb*) *white sugar* in a thick pan with the contents of a *small tin condensed milk*, add 200*g* (8 *oz*) *butter*, 1 *teaspoon vanilla essence* and 250*ml* (½ *pt*) *milk*. Bring it gently to the boil, stirring. Boil gently till it sets. To test drop a little in a cup of cold water when it should harden into toffee.

If set, pour it into a buttered tin. When cool, mark it in squares, break it up when cold. Store it in a tin.

In damp weather toffee soon becomes soft and sticky; some cooks wrap each piece in waxed paper before storing in a tin.

Kendal Mint Cake

This traditional white toffee is now also made in quantity by Atkinsons of Windermere and it is a source of quiet Cumbrian pride that some of it was carried up Everest by the British expedition that made the first-ever ascent of the world's highest peak. The recipe, like that for Buttered Sops, is from RECIPES OF LAKELAND.

Take 1 *lb white sugar,* ¼ *pt milk,* ½ *teaspoon or* 3 *drops peppermint essence.* Put the sugar and milk into a pan and heat it gently, stirring until the sugar melts, then boil it to the soft ball stage. Take it off the heat and add the peppermint essence. Now beat the mixture well until it is smooth and slightly setting, though still liquid. Pour it into a buttered tin but keep back one tablespoonful of the mixture, beat this until it grains, add this to the top of the mint cake when it is in the tin.

Russian Toffee

Russian Toffee is also called Butter Toffee or sometimes Swiss Toffee, perhaps because it is made with condensed milk which is called 'Swiss milk' by some people.

Bring to the boil 400*g* (1 *lb*) *soft brown sugar*, 200*g* (8 *oz*) *butter*, the contents of 1 *small tin of condensed milk* and 3 *tablespoons golden syrup* in a thick heavy pan, gently at first, stirring until the sugar melts. Then boil the toffee mixture gently, for about 25 minutes until it hardens in water. Pour it into a buttered tin. Mark it in squares before it is cold, so that it can later be divided into neat toffees.

FOR NUT TOFFEE, roast some unsalted almonds or peanuts. Put them in a buttered tin and pour the toffee over them. Mark it in squares as usual. Break it up when hard, and store the pieces in a tin.

Toffee Apples

In the old Northwich Market there used to be a man selling whirls of striped toffee from Liverpool which smelled not only of black treacle but vinegar and was called Peg's Leg, if I remember right. They sold old-fashioned toffee apples, too, when I was a child, but I was never allowed to have any for fear of ruining my teeth, and because 'you don't know where they've been'. But where could they have been when you think of it?

Wash and dry 12 *medium eating apples*. Take off the stalks and push a wooden skewer firmly into the stalk end of each apple. Put everything else into a large thick pan – 150*g* (6 *oz*) *golden syrup*, 300*g* (12 *oz*) *light brown soft sugar*, 125*ml* (¼ *pt*) *water* and 1 *teaspoon vinegar*. Heat it gently, stirring, until the sugar melts. Then bring it to the boil. Boil it briskly until a drop in cold water will snap cleanly – 143°C (290°F) on the sugar thermometer. Dip each apple in the toffee and twist it round with the help of the skewer so it is completely coated with toffee. Then dip it in cold water to set the toffee on the outside.

Stand the apples on a buttered tray. If they are not going to be eaten at once the toffee apples will have to be wrapped, as like most toffee, that on the outside of the apples will go sticky if left in the air.

Very popular at bazaars and jumble sales.

Treacle Toffee

This was always said to be very good for a tickling cough, and it was made in a small saucepan on the nursery fire. No toffee ever tastes so good as this now. If you were the one with a cough, or a bit feverish, you were allowed to stir it. Professional sweet-makers say toffee should never be stirred, as well-made toffee should look clear, not sugary, and stirring crystallizes it. No matter, we always stirred it, and it was almost worth having a cold for.

Stir 400*g* (1 *lb*) *brown sugar* gently in 125*ml* (¼ *pt*) *water* over a low heat until it melts, then add 50*g* (2 *oz*) *butter, a pinch of cream of tartar*, 100*g* (4 *oz*) *black treacle* and 100*g* (4 *oz*) *golden syrup*. Bring it to the boil and heat it, stirring from time to time so the bottom does not burn. Then when a few drops poured into cold water set hard and snap like an icicle when tested – it's done.

Pour the toffee at once into a well-buttered or well-greased tin. When cool and setting, mark it in squares. Turn it out when cold, break it up with a tack hammer. Store it in an airtight tin, otherwise it will go all sticky.

Plot Toffee

'Plot toffee' is the name given to treacle toffee in some parts of Yorkshire where – as elsewhere in the north of England – it is made for Bonfire Night on November 5th, Gunpowder Plot Night, or Guy Fawkes Day. Parkin is also eaten round the bonfire. In Swaledale, Yorkshire, they make a kind of treacle toffee for Bonfire Night which is pulled out with the hands like Mint Humbugs and twisted in long lengths – it is called Tom Trot.

XII
Gingerbread

Ashbourne Gingerbreads
Fairground Gingerbread
Gingerbread Husbands
Making Your Own Cutters
Grasmere Ginger Shortbread
Lancashire Gingerbread, Dark and Sticky
Plain Cumberland Gingerbread
Parkin or Parkins
Ginger Sandwich Cake
Wirksworth Thor Cakes

Gingerbread

Dried ginger was known in Europe even before Roman times. It was much used in the Middle Ages against the Black Death as it promotes sweating, which was then thought to be helpful. Almost every country in Europe has traditional spice cakes and honeybreads flavoured with ginger. There are recipes in the British Isles for ginger biscuits, cakes, parkins, gingersnaps, ginger pudding, ginger toast as well as ginger beer, ginger wine and dry ginger. In Corfu, which was a British protectorate during the early part of the nineteenth century, a traditional local drink named Tsintsinbirra, or ginger beer, is sold in the older cafés on the island. It is none other than that home-made ginger beer which delighted harvesters and country children a generation ago. We used to import crystallized ginger and stem ginger in ginger syrup from the Far East in pretty Chinese pots when it was virtually unknown on the Continent. Some of the tall Georgian silver sugar-casters were made originally for holding powdered ginger, which is still shaken over iced melon in England.

Medieval English gingerbread seems to have been a solid slab of honeycake like that still sold on fairgrounds in Central Europe. The gilt on it may have been real gold leaf. Food at court in Edward II's day was elaborately decorated – some Indian food is still garnished with gold and silver leaf. While the gingerbread was still hot from baking it was apparently brushed with egg whites and then the real gold leaf was laid on top. The egg white made it stick.

Ashbourne Gingerbreads

Ashbourne gingerbreads looks very much like ordinary biscuits until one tastes them and has another, and another. They are quite famous in some parts of Derbyshire and the Ashbourne Gingerbread Shop – a half-timbered establishment full of rich fruit loaves, wakes cakes and potted meat – at 26 St John Street in Ashbourne, is ready to post gingerbread all over the world. Mrs Macgibbon told me she has even sent the gingerbread gift boxes to Canada, in spite of the modern postal rates making them so much more expensive than they are in the shop. I tasted the local Wakes Cakes too, and could not stop eating them – as big as coffee saucers, flavoured with mace or nutmeg and bulging with currants. Nowadays they are made all the year round, not just in Wakes Week.

This is the traditional local recipe for the gingerbread: Cream 200*g* (8 *oz*) *butter* and 125*g* (5 *oz*) *caster sugar* until they are pale and fluffy. Sift in 250*g* (10 *oz*) *plain flour*, 2 *level teaspoons ground ginger* and *a pinch of salt.* Add 25*g* (1 *oz*) *finely-chopped peel.*

Knead this with the hands until it is a smooth dough. Roll it out with the hands into a long sausage about 2.5*cm* (1 *in*) thick. Cut it into lengths, 5cm (2 in) long, and put them on a lightly-greased baking sheet. Now flatten each roll a little with three fingers. Bake them in a moderate oven 180°C (350°F) Gas Mark 4 for about 20 minutes.

Fairground Gingerbread

Gingerbread used to be sold at fairs and some of the fairground operatives made a speciality of gingerbread 'husbands' which were shaped in wooden moulds, then baked and gilded. There are all kinds of gingerbread and parkin recipes up and down the country, from the very rich to the very simple. I had this recipe for fairground gingerbread from a Mrs Dorothy Watson. It was given to her by an 80-year-old aunt who died in about 1950. It is what used to be sold at country fairs in Yorkshire in the early part of the century.

Crumble 100*g* (4 *oz*) *butter or lard* into 800*g* (2 *lb*) *plain flour* mixed with 200*g* (8 *oz*) *brown sugar*, 50*g* (2 *oz*) *ground ginger*, 12*g* (½ *oz*) *ground caraway seeds.* Then stir into this 800*g* (2 *lb*) *black treacle* and 3 *very well-whisked eggs.* Last of all add 12*g* (½ *oz*) *bicarbonate of soda* dissolved in *a small cup of warm water*. Stir it briskly. Put it without delay in a well-greased shallow tin or in two tins, only half full to leave room for the gingerbread to rise. Put it in a moderate oven 180°C (350°F) Gas Mark 4 and bake it for 1½ hours.

When cold cut it up into thick squares.

Gingerbread Husbands

This recipe is enough for about twenty. The husbands should be stored in a tin until required for use.

Sift 400*g* (1 *lb*) *plain flour, a pinch salt, a level teaspoon bicarbonate of soda, a level dessertspoon ground ginger* and ½ *a level dessertspoon ground cinnamon* into a bowl. Mix well. Heat 100*g* (4 *oz*) *butter*, 200*g* (8 *oz*) *soft brown sugar* and 4 *tablespoons black treacle* gently in a pan, stirring until the treacle is runny and the sugar has melted. Let it cool slightly. Stir it into the flour mixture adding enough *milk* – about 1 tablespoon or less – to make a firm pastry-type dough. Chill it for 30 minutes or longer before rolling it out 6mm (¼ in) thick on a lightly-floured board.

Cut it into gingerbread husbands with a special cutter, or make a cardboard pattern of appropriate shape. Lay this on top of the gingerbread dough and cut round it with a sharp knife. Collect the small pieces of offcut dough, roll them out again and repeat. Lay the gingerbread husbands carefully on a lightly-buttered baking tray with the aid of two fish slices.

Put currants on them for eyes, nose and buttons. Bake them in a very moderate oven 170°C (325°F) Gas Mark 3 for about 15 minutes. Cool them on a wire tray or similar.

Making Your Own Cutters

I have made my own gingerbread cutters quite successfully by using a wooden block, about 15cm by 5cm by 5cm (6 in by 2 in by 2 in). Outline the shape of the 'man' or whatever on the block then hammer in a series of metal corrugated clips. They are shaped like this  and are about 2.5cm (1 in) long, they are thin enough to bend fairly easily. These clips are used on packing packs to draw the planks of wood together. You can sometimes find them in do-it-yourself shops.

Obviously your pattern should not be too elaborate, either for the clips or the dough. The crinkled edge of the dough when cooked is most decorative, but do make sure that all the clips are hammered level or your gingerbread shape will not cut cleanly.

Grasmere Ginger Shortbread

In Grasmere this shortbread is eaten sandwiched with ginger cream, though it can be cut in fingers and stored in a tin to eat plain. Grasmere is, of course, the heart of the Wordsworth country and a lively trade in ginger shortbread is carried on with tourists.

For the pastry: mix 200*g* (8 *oz*) *plain flour* with 100*g* (4 *oz*) *moist brown 'pieces' sugar*, this is important as white sugar won't make it. Add $\frac{1}{4}$ *teaspoon bicarbonate of soda*, 1 *teaspoon ground ginger* and *a small pinch of salt*. Rub in 100*g* (4 *oz*) *butter* until the mixture is like fine crumbs. Have ready a shallow dripping tin (or similar) lined with buttered foil. Empty the mixture into it, spreading it with your hands and pressing it very lightly together. Bake it in a moderate oven 180°C (350°F) Gas Mark 4 until lightly browned in about 45 minutes.

When cooked turn it out. If it is to be stored or eaten as plain ginger shortbread, cut it in fingers while still warm and lift it gently into the tin with a knife blade. If it is to be sandwiched in the orthodox manner, trim the edges and cut it in two while still hot. Add the filling when the cake is cold.

For the filling: beat 100*g* (4 *oz*) *icing sugar* and 50*g* (2 *oz*) *butter* to a cream, adding $\frac{1}{2}$ *teaspoon ground ginger, or a little chopped preserved stem ginger* and *a teaspoon of the syrup*. Spread it evenly on one piece of ginger shortbread, press the other in position on top. Dust with icing sugar.

Lancashire Gingerbread, Dark and Sticky

Melt 400*g* (1 *lb*) *butter* in a pan. Add 400*g* (1 *lb*) *black treacle*, 200*g* (8 *oz*) *soft dark brown sugar*, 500*ml* (1 *pt*) *milk* and *a tablespoon dark chunky bitter marmalade*. Stir it over a low heat until the sugar has melted, then let it cool. Meanwhile measure 200*g* (8 *oz*) *wholemeal flour* and 200*g* (8 *oz*) *selfraising flour* into a large bowl with 2 *teaspoons ground ginger* and 2 *teaspoons mixed spice* (not to be confused with allspice or Jamaica pepper – that used here is similar to the one for puddings). Add *half a level teaspoon bicarbonate of soda* and *a handful of sultanas*.

Beat up 3 *large eggs* and stir them into the flour mixture, gradually adding the warm butter mixture from the pan. Pour this cake into a deep baking tin lined with buttered paper. Bake it in a moderate oven 180°C (350°F) Gas Mark 4 for about 90 minutes. Cool it on a sieve and let the cake become quite cold before it is cut.

Plain Cumberland Gingerbread

This is a more economical recipe than the preceding one. Butter a Yorkshire pudding tin and line it with buttered foil. Mix 250*g* (10 *oz*) *flour* with ½ *teaspoon salt*, rub in 75*g* (3 *oz*) *lard*. Add 75*g* (3 *oz*) *sugar*, ½ *teaspoon bicarbonate of soda*, 2 *teaspoons ground ginger* and 25*g* (1 *oz*) *chopped candied peel*. Mix 125*ml* (¼ *pt*) *milk* with 100*g* (4 *oz*) *warm golden syrup* and 100*g* (4 *oz*) *warm black treacle*. Add *a beaten egg* then beat all this into the rest, mixing well. Pour it into the prepared Yorkshire pudding tin. Bake it in a moderately hot oven 190°C (375°F) Gas Mark 5 for 45–60 minutes.

Parkin or Parkins

Parkin or Parkins is the traditional spicy gingerbread made with oatmeal and black treacle which all the best people up north have on Guy Fawkes night. It should be made well beforehand as it takes at least a week to mature. It should not be kept in a tin for that makes it go dry, but will keep for a couple of months on a cool shelf, or in an old-fashioned bread crock if available.

Mix 125*g* (5 *oz*) *plain flour* with 400*g* (1 *lb*) *medium oatmeal* and *one teaspoon ground ginger*. Melt 125*g* (5 *oz*) *butter* or *lard* with 125*g* (5 *oz*) *brown sugar*, and 300*g* (12 *oz*) *black treacle*, stirring and not letting it get too hot. One easy way of weighing out black treacle or golden syrup without getting sticky is to equalize the balance of a basin on the scales, add a 300*g* (12 *oz*) weight and then, having warmed the treacle or syrup, pour it in until you get the right weight.

When the mixture in the pan has cooled a little add all this to the dry ingredients, stirring and mixing them with 125*ml* (¼ *pt*) *beer* and adding a little *milk* if need be, to make it more like thick batter than a cake dough. Have ready a well-greased and floured roasting tin, or Yorkshire pudding tin, the bottom lined with foil or with greaseproof paper.

Tip in the mixture. Bake it in a moderate oven 180°C (350°F) Gas Mark 4 for 45 to 60 minutes or until it is firm to the touch. It does not rise much. The alcohol in the beer is given off in cooking so the Parkin is not at all inebriating. Cut it in squares as required.

Parkin is eaten all through November in the north and is very good for lunch with a piece of cheese. In Cheshire the village shops used to be full of it at this time of the year – big black slabs of Parkin lying on the counters cheek by jowl with pink and yellow gobstoppers and mint humbugs. In Cheshire, country children still go 'souling' in late October, singing from house to house. This has nothing to do with Christmas, they are given a little bun or 'soul' cake in exchange. These are always made on 28 October and meant to be eaten on 2 November, a time of ghosts and witchcraft. 'A soul cake, a soul cake. Have mercy on all Christian souls' one chants as one eats it. It is all thick with tradition. Lancashire Parkin used to be called Harcake or Soul Mass cake and was originally associated with All Souls' Day on 2 November – not Guy Fawkes. Har is the Norse name for the pagan god Odin. It all goes back to the pagan winter festival. Derbyshire folk still make Thor or Thar cakes, a sort of Parkin with candied peel in it, for bonfire night.

Ginger Sandwich Cake

This is made in two lined and well-buttered sponge sandwich tins. When cool, it is put together with whipped cream in the middle and sieved caster sugar or icing sugar on top.

Cream 50*g* (2 *oz*) *butter*, add 2 *tablespoons warm golden syrup* and 1 *tablespoon warm black treacle.* Mix well and then add 2 *beaten eggs*, one by one and alternately with 200*g* (8 *oz*) *selfraising flour* sifted with *a heaped teaspoon ground ginger* and *a teaspoon ground cinnamon.*

Mix this to a smooth consistency with 125*ml* (¼ *pt*) *milk.* Pour it into 2 prepared sandwich tins. Bake them in a hot oven 200°C (400°F) Gas Mark 6 for 30 to 40 minutes.

When the cakes are cool, sandwich them with whipped cream mixed with chopped crystallized or stem ginger, or with a filling of 4 tablespoons sifted icing sugar mixed to a smooth cream with some syrup from a jar of stem ginger. Add a little stem ginger, chopped. Dust the top with sifted icing sugar.

Wirksworth Thor Cakes

For festival days Derbyshire villagers prepare great screens, some of them 5–6 metres (16–20 feet) high, tighly packed with flowers to form a floral mosaic. These are then carried out and set up by the local well. Those done at Wirksworth are breathtaking. 'There's nowt like our well-dressing!' they say locally. No one knows how the custom began, nor when, nor why. The subjects are usually religious and to do with water. Before the last war there were pearly gates and shining paths to Heaven made of close-packed rice which is said to have gleamed like mother-of-pearl in the sunset.

At Wirksworth, as at Bonsall, the rule was always 'only things that grow'. Not a glass eye was permitted in portraying even kings, queens and saints. In the 1940s there were men who had sacrificed a week's pay and their annual holiday to 'dress the wells', as it is called. Rivalry was then intense both between villagers and competitors. None of the wells was ever dressed the same way twice. The pictures, treatment and even the flowers used were always different. Workers carried on all through the night so that the flowers would be fresh for the opening day. At Youlgrave the magnificent victory screen done by Mr W. Clarke the blacksmith was talked about for years. It showed Britannia, having burst the chains of war, looking with joy and hope towards a gorgeous sun of freedom made from marigold petals. Mr Clarke used to do local views in oils in his spare time.

Wirksworth is a bleak little hill town with steep winding streets and wide views of a green valley. Huge pictures in flowers or flower petals are done for their well dressing traditionally on Whit Monday, with maypole dancing in the market place. Of course nearly all Derbyshire villages have special cakes for Wakes Week but Wirksworth makes Thor cakes as well for 5 November.

FOR WIRKSWORTH THOR CAKES Mix 400*g* (1 *lb*) *fine oatmeal*, 400*g* (1 *lb*) *plain flour*, 400*g* (1 *lb*) *sugar*, 50*g* (2 *oz*) *chopped peel*, 1 *teaspoon coriander seeds* and 1 *teaspoon ground ginger*. Add 2 *teaspoons baking powder* and 1 *teaspoon salt*. Mix well.

Rub in 300*g* (12 *oz*) *butter*. Add 400*g* (1 *lb*) *warmed black treacle*. Knead the dough a little and roll it out fairly thin. Cut it in large rounds. Place them on a greased oven sheet and bake in a moderate oven 180°C (350°F) Gas Mark 4 for about 20 minutes.

Index of Recipes

Alice's Rich Beef Pie, 39
Annie Funnell's Scratching Pie, 57
Apples, Toffee Apples, 141–2
Ashbourne Gingerbreads, 147–8

Bacon and Cow-Heel:
  Jellies, 76
  Pudding, 53
Bacon and Egg Pies, 51–2
Bacon and Red Lentils, 52
Bacon Saucers, 51
Bakewell 'Pudding', 104
Balmbra's Pudding, 37–8
Batter, 51
Beef:
  Balmbra's Pudding, 37–8
  Lancashire Beef and Cow-heel Tart, 76
  Old-fashioned Souse, 79
  Panakelty, 41–2
  Pie, 39
  Pot Roast and Forcemeat Balls, 35–6
  Roast Rump with Yorkshire Pudding, 32–5
  Rump Steak and Onions, 40
  Salted Dry-Fried Steaks, 40
  Sausages, 41
  Stewed Rump, 36–7
  Yorkshire Cobbler, 38–9
Binjean (Manx Junket), 94
Biscuit Dough, to freeze, 118
Biscuits:
  Grannie's, 117–18
  Ratafias or macaroons, 95–6
Bilberries, 101–2
Bilberry Pie, 103
Bilberry Tart, 102–3
Black Puddings, 48–50
  with Tatie Pot, 65
Blackcurrant Fool, 92–3
Boudins, 48–50
Brawns:
  Beef, 75
  Harvest, 77
  Oxtail, 77
  and Pea Wack, 77–8
Brandy Snaps, 93–4
Bread:
  Fancy, 122
  Yorkshire Yule Loaf, 122
Breadcrumbs, Soft White, 107
Butterscotch, 139

Cabbage, Pickled Red, 63
Cakes:
  Cut-and-Come-Again, 124
  Derbyshire Oatcakes, 123
  Eccles, 113–14
  Family Fruit, 125–6
  Ginger Sandwich, 153
  Goosnargh, 113–14
  Plain Sponge Sandwich, 119–20
  Rock, 118–19
  Roll-up Havacake, 123–4
  Seed, 120
  Simnel, 120–22
  Wirksworth Thor, 153–4
  Yorkshire Oven-Bottom, 117
  see also Gingerbread

Cannon-Ball Pudding, 94
Char, 27–8
Cheese:
  Cheshire, 83–4
  Cream, to make, 85–6
  Derbyshire, 86
  Lancashire, 84–5
  Wensleydale, 87–8
Cheese Dishes:
  Cheese, Bacon and Onion Pie, 85
  Cheese and Onion Pie, 87
  Pan Haggerty, 88
  Scones, 86
Cheesecakes, 108–9
Cheshire Cheese, 83–4
  to pot, 84
Chicken:
  Christmas Pork and Chicken, 47–8
  To roast: a hen, 68–9; an old hen in dripping, 62
Chip Butties, 42–3
Christmas Pork and Chicken, 47–8
Cod:
  Boiled, with Melted Butter, 19–20
  Cold Steaks in Lemon Sauce, 17
  Scarborough Cod, 19
Cow-heel, 76, 79
Cow-heel and Bacon Pudding, 53
Cow-heel, Old-fashioned Souse, 79
Cow-heel, Oxtail and Shin of Beef, 33
Crab, Home-made Potted, 18
Crokky Pies, 61–2
Crumpets, 114–15
Cumberland:
  Gingerbread, 151
  Sauce, 133–4
  Sausages, 48
Curd Tarts, 108–9
Cut-and-Come-Again Cake, 124

Derbyshire Oatcakes, 123
Doncaster Butterscotch, 139
Dripping Toast, 42–3
Duke of Cambridge Tart, 104–5
Durham Pikelets, 116

Eccles Cakes, 113–14
Egg Sauce, 25
Everton Toffee, 139–40

Farce au Gratin, 68
Farmhouse Game Pie, 71–2
Fidget (Fitchett) Pie, 117
Fish, *see* Cod, Crab, etc.
Fish Cakes, 21
Fish Hot-Pot, 23–4
Flat-Fish and Shrimps, 23
Forcemeat Balls, 36
Fruit Cake, 125–6

Game Pie, Farmhouse, 71–2
Ginger Snaps, 93–4
Gingerbread:
  Ashbourne, 147–8
  Fairground, 148–9
  Ginger Sandwich Cake, 153
  Grasmere Ginger Shortbread, 150
  Husbands, 149
  Lancashire, Dark and Sticky 151
  Parkin(s), 151–3
  Plain Cumberland, 151

Gingerbread – *contd.*
Wirksworth Thor Cakes, 153–4
Gingerbread Cutters, Making, 149–50
Gooseberry Sauce, 134
Goosnargh Cakes, 114
Grannie Biscuits, 117–18
Grasmere Ginger Shortbread, 150
Griddle Scones, 115–16
Grouse, 67–8
Roast Yorkshire, 68

Ham, 50
Ham and Pease Pudding, 53–4
Ham and Tripe Pie, 67
Haslet (Aislet), 55–6
Herb Pudding, 31
Herrings, 15
Baked, 21–2
Fried, 25
Grilled, 25
Honeycomb Mould, 92
Hot-Pot:
Fish, 23–4
Lancashire, 62–3
Hull Fish Cakes, 21
Humbugs, 137

Icing for Pie Crust, 103

Jams and Jellies:
Bilberry and Rhubarb, 129
Elderflower and Gooseberry, 130
Marrow and Ginger, 130–31
Marrow and Pineapple, 131
Rhubarb, Ginger and Chopped Peel, 132
Junket, Manx, 94

Kendal Mint Cake, 140–41
Kippers, 16–17
Kipper Soufflé, 20

Lancashire:
Beef and Cow-heel Tart, 76
Cheese, 84–5
Gingerbread, 151
Hot-Pot, 62–3
Lemon Curd Tarts, 105
Lentil Soup, 52–3
Lentils and Bacon, 52
Lobster, Hot with Butter, 16

Macaroons, 95–6
Mackerel, 24
Marzipan, 122
Mealie Puddings, 50
Mint Cake, 140–41
Mock Jugged Hare, 35–6
Moorland Tart, 106
Muffins, 114–15
Mustard Sauce, 24; traditional Yorkshire, 50
Mutton Saucer Pies, 63–4

North Country Gooseberry Sauce, 134
Northumberland Ham and Leek Pastry, 57–8
Nut Toffee, 141

Oatcakes, 123
Old-fashioned Velvet Cream, 98
Old Middleham Tart, 105–6
Omble Chevalier, 27–8
Onion Sauce, 70–71
Oxtail, Yorkshire Potted, 79–80

Pail Dinners, 61–2
Pan Haggerty, 88

Panakelty, 41–2
Parkin(s), 151–3
Pastry:
  Biscuit Crust, 110
  Extra Crust, 110
  Shortcrust, 109–10
Pasty, Northumberland Ham and Leek, 57–8
Pea Wack and Brawn, 77–8
Pease Pudding and Boiled Ham, 53–4
Perch, Fried, 26
Pestle, 78–9
Pickled Red Cabbage, 63
Pickles, Orange, 131–2
Pies, Savoury:
  Alice's Rich Beef, 39
  Annie Funnell's Scratching Pie, 57
  Bacon and Egg, 51–2
  Cheese, Bacon and Onion, 85
  Cheese and Onion, 87
  Farmhouse Game, 71–2
  Fidget or Fitchett, 117
  Mutton Saucer, 63–4
  Rabbit, 71
  Shepherd's, 64–5
Pies, Sweet:
  Bilberry, 103
Pig's Trotters, 78–9
Pikelets, 116
Pork:
  Annie Funnell's Scratching Pie, 57
  Black Puddings, 48–50
  Christmas Pork and Chicken 47–8
  Haslet or Aislet, 55–6
  Northumberland Ham and Leek Pasty, 57–8
  Pestle, 78–9
  Savoury Ducks, 56
  White Puddings, 50
  Yorkshire Savoury Pudding, 54–5
Puddings, Savoury:
  Bacon and Cow-heel, 53
  Balmbra's, 37–8
  Yorkshire Savoury, 54–5
Puddings, Sweet:
  Bakewell, 104
  Blackcurrant Fool, 92–3
  Brandy or Ginger Snaps, 93–4
  Cannon-Ball Pudding, 94
  Honeycomb Mould, 92
  Old-fashioned Velvet Cream, 98
  Prunes in Port, 95
  Ratafia with Wine Sauce, 96
  Roly Poly, 97
  Skipton Pudding, 97
  Spotted Dog, 97
  Wet Nellies, 94–5

Rabbit:
  Boiled and Smothered in Onions, 70–71
  Pie, 71
  Sandwiches, 71
Raspberry Vinegar, 134
Ratafias, 95–6
Ratafia Pudding with Wine Sauce, 96
Red Lentils:
  with Bacon, 52
  Soup, 52–3
Rock Cakes, 118–19
Roll-Up Havacake, 123–4
Roly-Poly Pudding, 97
Rum Butter, 132–3

Salmon, 25–7
Potted, 27
Scouse, 25
Sandwiches, Rabbit, 71
Sauces:
Blackberry Vinegar, 134
Cumberland, 133–4
Egg, 25
Mustard, 24, 50
North Country Gooseberry, 134
Raspberry Vinegar, 134
Wine, 96
Sausages:
Beef, 41
Cumberland Pork, 48
Sausages and Tripe, 67
Savoury Ducks, 56
Scones, Cheese, 86
Shepherd's Pie, 64–5
Shrimps and Flat-Fish, 23
Shrimps, Potted, 22
Simnel Cake, 120–22
Singin' Hinnies, 115–16
Skipton Pudding, 97
Soufflé, Kipper, 20
Soup, Red Lentil, 52–3
Souse, Old-fashioned, 79
Spiced Vinegar, 63
Sponge Sandwich, 119–20
Spotted Dog, 97
Staithes Herrings, Baked, 21–2
Steak and Onions, 40
Steak, Salted Dry-fried, 40
Suet Pudding Stuffed with Mushrooms, 31
Suety Jack, 97
Sugar Thermometers, 133
Sweets and Toffee:
Aunt Maggie's Cough Candy, 139
Buttered Sops, 138
Cinder Toffee, 138–9
Doncaster Butterscotch, 139
Everton Toffee, 139–140
Kendal Mint Cake, 140–41
Milk Toffee, 140
Mint Humbugs, 138
Nut Toffee, 141
Pink Sugar Mice, 140
Plot Toffee, 143
Russian Toffee, 141
Toffee Apples, 141–2
Treacle Toffee, 142–3

Tart, Savoury:
Lancashire Beef and Cow-heel, 76
Tarts, Sweet:
Bilberry, 102–3
Curd, 108–9
Duke of Cambridge, 104–5
Lemon Curd, 105
Moorland, 106
Old Middleham, 105–6
Treacle, 106–7
Westmorland Threedecker, 107–8
Wilfra, 108
Tatie Pot with Black Puddings, 65
Toast, 42–3
Tripe, 65–6
with parsley, 66
and Sausages, 67
Tripe and Ham Pie, 67
Thermometers, 133
Toffee, *see* Sweets and Toffee
Treacle Tart, 106–7
Trout, Fried, 26
Tweed Salmon, 25–6

Venison roasted in foil, 72
Vinegar:
  Blackberry, 134
  Raspberry, 134
  Spiced, 63

Wensleydale Cheese, 87–8
Westmorland Threedecker, 107–8
Wet Nellies, 94–5
Whitby Lobsters, 16
White Puddings, 50
Wilfra Tarts, 108
Wine Sauce, 96
Wirksworth Thor Cakes, 153–4

Yorkshire:
  Cheesecakes, 108–9
  Cobbler, 38–9
  Oven-Bottom Cake, 116
  Pikelets, 116
  Potted Oxtail, 79–80
  Pudding, 33–4
    with Mushrooms, 34–5
    Traditional, 34
  Savoury Pudding, 54–5
  Seed Cake, 120